LETS
GO
PUBLISH!

LETS GO United States of America!

Democrat Secret for Power & Winning Elections

Open borders & amnesty eventually add millions of new Democrat Voters

Kevin McAleenan, the commissioner of U.S. Customs and Border Protection, said the agency detained 4,100 illegal aliens in just one day in March, 2019. It was the largest number of illegal aliens to be arrested in one day in over ten years but it has since been surpassed. Houston, we certainly do have a problem. Like it or not, it is an emergency!

In addition, border arrests skyrocketed to over 100,000 in the same month. Why? Because Democrats refuse to change the law and Customs and Border Patrol detention facilities are overwhelmed. They cannot house the surge of illegal aliens pouring over the Southern border. Congress won't solve the problem because it is part of the problem. It gains from the border problem remaining a problem, Otherwise, it would be solved already.

As difficult as it is for good, hard working Democrats to believe, our government is working to keep us all poor. They are lying and they are passing legislation that can only help somebody from another country beat out an American for the few jobs that exist in America. It's not the President's fault. All fault lies with our cowardly, greedy, corrupt Congress. Moreover, their power/election and donor suck-up strategies are making it worse.

Worse than that, once the illegal foreign nationals get the American jobs, our legislators turn their back on doing anything to remove them from the country or the job. They are rooting for foreigners instead of Americans. Big money people want to get the hourly wage down so low, bread and water will be a luxury. Our legislators in Congress and the Democrat Presidencies approved these actions. Any questions?

Secretary Neilson sent Congress a few salient letters as the crisis worsened on the border. The silence from the corrupt press was deafening. It looks like Congress cares only about Congress and what they can take from America. Only the people can make this better and we must.

You will love this book folks as it shows exactly what the problem is and it shows how Democrats and RINO Republicans are hell bent on not permitting solutions to pass for the good of the people. The people can do better. It looks like we have to find a big broom and wholesale sweep out this bad batch in Congress today. If we don't act, we will become the problem as our country is destroyed by the inaction of our Congress.

LETS GO PUBLISH

BRIAN W. KELLY

Democrat Secret for Power & Winning Elections

Copyright © 2019 Brian W. Kelly   Publisher/ Editor, Brian P. Kelly
Democrat Secret for Power & Winning Elections   Author, Brian W. Kelly

Open borders & amnesty eventually add millions of new Democrat Voters

Referenced Material : *The information in this book has been obtained through personal and third-party observations, interviews, and copious research. Where unique information has been provided or extracted from other sources, those sources are acknowledged within the text of the book itself or at the end of the chapter in the Sources Section. Thus, there are no formal footnotes nor is there a bibliography section. Any picture that does not have a source was taken from various sites on the Internet with no credit attached. If resource owners would like credit in the next printing, please email publisher.*

Published by: .... LETS GO PUBLISH!
Publisher & Editor: ....Brian P. Kelly
Mail Location: ....   P.O. Box 621, Wilkes-Barre, PA
Email: ....info@letsgopublish.com
Web site.. www.letsgopublish.com

Library of Congress Copyright Information Pending
Book Cover Design by Brian W. Kelly, Editing by Brian P. Kelly

ISBN Information: The International Standard Book Number (ISBN) is a unique machine-readable identification number, which marks any book unmistakably. The ISBN is the clear standard in the book industry. 159 countries and territories are officially ISBN members. The Official ISBN For this book is on the outside cover:
978-1-947402-80-5

The price for this work is :									$12.95
USD									
10	9	8	7	6	5	4	3	2	1

Release Date: April 2019

Dedication

I dedicate this book

To my wonderful and beautiful wife Patricia.

She encourages my work and she supports all of my efforts with all the charm of the lady, which she is.

Thank you Pat!

Acknowledgments

I would like to thank many people for helping me in this effort.

I appreciate all the help that I have received in putting this book together as well as all of my other 195 published books.

My printed acknowledgments had become so large that book readers "complained" about going through too many pages to get to page one of the text.

And, so to permit me more flexibility, I asked Wiley Ky Eyely, a local mystic, and an editor exemplare. Ms. Ky Eyeley said it was OK to put my acknowledgment list online, and it continues to grow to this day. Believe it or not, it once cost about a dollar more to print each book.

Thank you and God bless you all for your help.

Please check out www.letsgopublish.com to read the latest version of my heartfelt acknowledgments updated for this book. Click the bottom of the Main menu!

Thank you all!

.

Table of Contents

Preface:

Congress has been trying to pull a fast one on Americans probably from the very first election. In the recent past, the knaves got together with a "bipartisan" group of eight and this gang of eight tyrants' put together an amnesty plan that was designed to kill America. RINO Republicans joined with voter-grubbing Democrats to buffalo the people.

If it passed under Obama, there would not have been any jobs left; but worse than that, there would be no more America. Even today, our only hope is Donald Trump as Congress has checked out of the game and nobody is in the on-deck-circle. When they did play ball, Congress was in it for themselves.

One day if Congress has its way, our country will be owned and overrun by illegal foreign nationals from Mexico and China. Americans are too trusting. We will be the saps paying illegal foreign national interlopers to live here for free. If you think things are bad for your kids now, wait until the legislation from the most corrupt politicians in America is rammed down everybody's throats. Don't worry about your representative, he or she will be exempted.

If you want foreigners to be voting in American elections, and you want newly minted citizens to be taking American jobs, and you want the average wage in America to keep going down, down, down, whoa oha oh (as in the Righteous brothers); and you want Congress to consider changing our national language from English to Mandarin, and you want to pay the cost of welfare cash and food and housing and medical for the new owners of America; and you want China and Russia to be the only superpowers left in the world, then please encourage your legislators in the HOUSE to quickly bring back and pass the old Senate's gang of eight tyrants' plan so that we can quickly move forth with the destruction of America the beautiful—and the once grand. Yes, this situation is that severe!

Look at the border if you have the guts. The mainstream press does not present the truth as they lie by design and the Democrats swear to their lies. If you want the truth about the border, and about who's coming to take your house and your job, please read Chapter 2 and see how Kirstjen Nielson, our terrific former Homeland Security Secretary suppliantly requested our Congress to do what only they can do—their jobs. Don't blame Trump if they do not. Expect nothing as Congress thinks that it is now independent of the people.

Your author, Brian W. Kelly monitors this stuff for us and even his wife thanks him for that most of the time. He is one of America's most outspoken and eloquent conservative spokesmen. He is the author of *Saving America, Taxation Without Representation, Obama's Seven Deadly Sins, Kill the EPA, Jobs! Jobs! Jobs!, Cowardly Congress*, and many other books on Amazon, Kindle, Barnes & Noble and others.

Like many Americans just like you, Brian is fed up with a stifling progressive liberal agenda in Washington that places the needs of illegal foreign national interlopers in front of the needs of Americans. You know you will get the straight scoop when you read a non-fiction Kelly book from amazon.com/author/brianwkelly.

Brian wrote this book to help Americans know that all members of Congress are failing the American people but even he admits Democrats are despicable in what they do for their personal greed even though they know it hurts America. Democrat donors want power and power comes with voting and the donor push for illegal voters is understandable but it is disheartening that our Congress would choose to sell us out rather than do their jobs.

Kelly shows us all what we can do to recognize the stains of our Congress and what we must do to either replace them all (throw the bums out) or force our government to regain control of our borders, ensure our national security, keep our culture, enforce our laws, protect American jobs, and keep all Americans from being overwhelmed by illegal foreign nationals with no allegiance to the USA.

Like you, Kelly is frustrated with the devastation that illegal immigration inflicts on law-abiding Americans and likewise he finds the destitution brought upon the illegal class by corporate America to be the greatest sin of all. He has read the intelligence reports, has researched and written about the topic for years, and he knows how intolerable illegal immigration can be within our neighborhoods.

He has written ten books about illegal immigration and he likes to call his solution comprehensible and sane. It has two parts and for those two parts, Kelly has written two different books with two separate solutions. Besides the border wall, which is a must, the problem with 60 million illegal interlopers is solved within the pages of these two books. You'll love them.

1. Pay to Go https://www.amazon.com//dp/1947402145
2. Resident Visa https://www.amazon.com/dp/194740217X

Few books are a must-read but *Democrat Secret for Power & Winning Elections* will quickly appear at the top of America's most read list.

About the Author

Brian W. Kelly retired as an Assistant Professor in the Business Information Technology (BIT) program at Marywood University, where he also served as the IBM i and midrange systems technical advisor to the IT faculty. Kelly designed, developed, and taught many college and professional courses. He is also a contributing technical editor to a number of IT industry magazines, including "The Four Hundred" and "Four Hundred Guru" published by IT Jungle.

Kelly is a former IBM Senior Systems Engineer and he has been a candidate for US Congress and the US Senate from Pennsylvania. He also ran for Mayor in his home town. He has an active information technology consultancy. He is the author of 196 books (including this one) and numerous articles. His articles are all non-fiction and range are typically about current IT topics or generally conservative thought. Kelly is a frequent speaker at COMMON, IBM conferences, and other technical conferences, & user group meetings across the US. Ask him to talk at your next TEA Party Rally. He knows how to work a crowd.

Over the past twenty years, Brian Kelly has become one of America's most outspoken and eloquent conservative protagonists. Besides No Amnesty! No Way!; Kelly is the author of Taxation Without Representation, Obama's Seven Deadly Sins, Healthcare Accountability, Kill the EPA, Jobs! Jobs! Jobs!, Saving America, RRR, The US Immigration Fix, and other conservative books. Endorsed by the Independence Hall Tea Party in 2010, Kelly ran for Congress against a 13-term Democrat and, took no campaign contributions, spent just $4500, and as a virtual unknown, he captured 17% of the vote—www.briankellyforcongress.com. Kelly then supported Republican challenger Lou Barletta, a conservative leader on immigration policy, and helped him win a resounding victory in the general election. Mr. Kelly also ran a write-in campaign for the US Senate v Bob Casey Jr. in 2012.

Chapter 1 Dems Know More Border-Crossings Mean More Democrats.

The Secret of Political Power – Voters

As you can deduce from the title of this book, Democrats have learned the secret for gaining political power. They have it deeply ingrained in their souls that open borders and amnesty eventually will add millions of new Democrat voters.

That one benefit alone from an anti-American safety strategy on the southern border will help Democrats in winning elections. You can take that to the bank as the Democrats bank on a future not too far away that will provide them with the amnesty, they need to amass many new citizens to bolster the election tallies for the Democrat Party.

Lawrence Lessig, a Harvard Law Professor writes as a caution to us all: "There is nothing more dangerous than a government of the many controlled by the few." When Democrats ask themselves if they believe in the same stuff their leaders preach, it is tough to believe they answer themselves in the affirmative.

Never, ever forget that Trump got the overwhelming amount of the religious conservative vote, but he did not run on social and religious conservative themes. Lest we forget, it was the unrelenting hostility of the Democratic Party to religious conservatives that drove many into Trump's arms.

Democrats today think the strategy of alienating their constituency, especially white male voters, and catering to those who are here illegally, will eventually pay off in more election victories. It makes no sense to me. As a white male myself as well as a registered Democrat, I think it is pretty stupid but I feel unwelcome by the Party nonetheless.

I do think Americans must pay attention to the plight at our borders and the millions here in the country for both safety reasons and because the Democrats are ready to damn long-standing American culture and tradition for their ultimate victory. *Whitey* has already becoming an endangered species in the Democrat Party. The Constitution is becoming the least favorite document of the democrat Party.

Can Democrats be conservative?

Everybody thinks of themselves as something. When I was twenty-one, fresh out of King's College as a Data Processing major, getting ready to work for IBM in Utica, New York, I registered to vote as an Independent. I did not like politics and the term independent and I were in synch.

I was unaware at the time about Pennsylvania election laws. By being registered Independent, I was in essence excluded from voting in the PA Primary Election. Two years later when IBM transferred me to my home state of Pennsylvania and I temporarily moved in with mom and pop, my father and I often discussed political affiliations. He had been a Democrat all his life and he took issue with anybody in PA being an Independent. After consideration, I changed my registration to Democrat and have been registered with the Party since 1971.

Both my dad and I became disenchanted with the Democrat Party when Jimmy Carter became President and inflation soared to 21%.

The last time either of us felt good enough to vote for a Democrat was for Bob Casey Sr. as Governor of PA. for the second time in 1990. Neither of us developed a love for Bob Casey, Jr., now Senator from PA because he is more of the new-style *anything-goes* Democrat than our type of man.

So, here I am in 2019 continuing in my forty-ninth year as a registered Democrat. Yet, I feel like more like a conservative; a nationalist; and a populist—without a real Party. I am nothing close to being a liberal progressive socialist. I know I do not belong in the Democrat Party but with so many RINOs and wimps in the Republican Party, I do not belong there either.

So, I have decided that my beliefs and not my label matter. However, I do recall the days when my dad was a loyal Democrat and then I became a loyal Democrat. But, way back then, the Democrats were indeed the party of the people. They were not faking it. Today, the Democrats have left folks like my dad and myself far behind in their wake.

Like you, perhaps, I hope one day to join a party such as *The John Doe Party* or *The American Party*. I'd join tomorrow if they existed. That will happen when those with the where-with-all find the spirit to form a new political party. When that Happens, I hope to join like-minded members of the Democrat, Republican, Libertarian, and Green Parties to form a party with the beliefs of all John Does who also have a deep love for America and its values.

Until then, I am content to have a voter's registration card that simply permits me to vote and it signifies nothing about my ideology. That is why for today, I am OK being a registered Democrat.

I find myself as a citizen of a truly exceptional country. Yet, even here in America all is not perfect. As bad as it may be, however, most Americans never expected the Democrats to begin to take it out on the country and on God.

Donald Trump may annoy people but he does not annoy me as I see him as one of our greatest Presidents—even perhaps greater than Reagan. He loves America like most of us, and in all things from jobs to trade to border protection, he thinks like most Americans. The President is well on his way to making America great again. And, that as we all feel it, is wonderful.

No leader in the Free World has the chutzpah of Donald J. Trump. I am ever so pleased that he uses his guts and grit to help America and Americans. In their stupid belief that Trump stole the election from Hillary Clinton, pigheaded Democrats are obsessed with hurting our President, and all those who have ever supported him. They look stupid damning Trump rather than doing their jobs in Congress. They don't care if they lay waste the notion of God and they trample on the American people in so doing.

While they are at it, for some inane reason they are also pleased to hurt all white males who do not pledge allegiance to the Democrat Party. They worship diversity as long as white males are not included in the diverse group. Ironically, too many white males are busy being good Democrats to notice.

They do not believe they have been abandoned. If they realized it, the Democrats would already be a small dot on the spectrum of political parties that have been collected in the dustbin of history. I do not think Democrats can get by as a Party with no white males in their group but that does not seem to bother them at all.

We see it everywhere and we see Democrats using their best weapon, *the lie*, to convince the people the Democrat Party, and not God is the Way, the Truth, and the Light. That of course is their biggest lie.

As a conservative populist nationalist, I believe in the country as founded—as a representative republic adhering to the Constitution—acknowledging that Amendments had to be added to the original document in order to remedy shortcomings. We all know that the political, cultural and legal situation at the time of founding (slavery) needed a bit of work in that area.

Having said that, because the founders were imperfect, does that make the document (Constitution) itself imperfect? Just like the Bible, written on parchment by man is not written perfectly, the precepts contained within the Bible are still as perfect as possible.

So also, the document known as the US Constitution is the greatest declaration and compact for a free society in the history of mankind. Much like parents don't (in general) disown their children simply because they are not perfect, we should not abolish the Constitutional form of government and national history just because the founders and subsequent leaders were flawed human beings. Yet, even though it would destroy our country, that is exactly what Democrats want to do.

From new calls to abolish the electoral college (because Hillary didn't win that part of the election of course) to taking down historical statues, to redefining everything from basic pronouns to gender and biology, the Left is on a tear to completely upend the American system, and with it, the societal norms that provide the foundations for a reasonably cohesive society – family, culture, language.

Most people are like me and we no longer believe in the Democrat Party. Unlike me and many others, not enough Registered Democrats look inward at their Party and call it out as being anti-God and anti-American. They all need to be braver and say it like it is.

It's not new of course, this has been going on for a long time, decades in fact, but the election of Trump sent them completely insane. There has been a warp-speed effort to change America and now they're not even trying to hide it. Heretofore actions have been being taken— stealthily, ploddingly, and even strategically but they were always been denied when revealed, and often with devastating unintended consequences.

A recent example of ideology trumping logic for instance—if accused of trying to undermine the judicial system with lax enforcement of punishment for delinquent kids, the cry was no, you're just being paranoid, (and of course racist) we're just trying to make things 'fair'—you know, the kind of 'fairness' which kept Nicolas Cruz out of jail or an institution for his multiple offenses under Obama's 'Promise Program'? Look how that turned out.

Others, such as holding school's hostage over Title 9 funding over transgender bathroom use or using Title 9 campus 'sexual assault guidance' to deprive male students of their constitutional right to due process and destroying their lives without recompense? You and I could go on and on. It makes no sense but nonetheless Democrats seem hell-bent on destroying their party.

Whether it's refusing to include curricula which includes the study of one religion (Christianity) while allowing the study of others (Islam, Buddhism), or punishing free speech and belief, the school system, run overwhelmingly by the Left, liberals have so successfully indoctrinated our kids and by default the society at large, that I'm not sure it will be possible to undo it. Hitler knew this – get the kids and you get the future. Before he failed big time, Hitler was way too successful. We can avoid that in America if we stay awake.

Trump did not cause this insanity of course. It has been around since long before he ran for President as a Republican. He was ballyhooed breathlessly by the Left in fact, (when they thought he was a Democrat). But wealth is wealth, after all, and they like rich, powerful, famous people, so they went along.

Trump has always been Trump. By taking them on like nobody before him, he helped reveal their insanity and hypocrisy, and their utter contempt for the American people. And for that matter, he revealed it in a large segment of the right as well. What happened to the Republicans when they were needed by conservatives? –MIA RINOS!

Make no mistake about it, America, the Left is coming after you and me and everybody else until they get us. We represent everything they hate: our guns, our prayers, our values, even our thoughts. And of course, most of all, our vote! And yes, when I refer to 'America', I'm referring to you, because the small sliver of 'reasonable' Democrats that might remain are rendered more irrelevant every day.

When they wake up to the fact that this Socialism Frankenstein that they've enabled to grow and fester will eventually turn on them in due time, it may be too late. We saw it happen in a recently scheduled Women's March—the one promoted by the America-hating Linda Sarsour who declared 'jihad' against President Trump. It was cancelled in California because organizers felt it would be 'too white'. Democrats do not like "white," other than at the ballot box.

Only we the America-loving Deplorables stand in their way. Why? Lots of reasons. Perhaps the biggest reason is that we hold to the intractable defense of the Constitution. We refuse to submit to their insane and ever-changing but always perverse cultural mores. We insist on real, not regulated Free Speech. Perhaps that most of all—for Free Speech equals free thought and Democrats certainly cannot have that.

No folks, Leftists are not hiding it anymore. Therefore, what elected Republicans and conservatives do during these next two years, as well as whether the average citizen learns what is at stake, will determine the direction of this country for ages, perhaps forever. With the influx of new Democrat voters arriving in caravans from Third-World countries, the demographics are in their favor. And so, we will soon have a compliant, uneducated (and overwhelmingly Democrat) future voter base, content to depend on the government, thus keeping them in perpetual power.

It's a win-win for both R and D in the Swamp too, for it enables the Republicans to get their cheap labor. Neither really cares about John or Jane Doe, just their donor base. Without our representatives who sold out a long time ago, we are all on our own. We do have a great leader and 63 million or more fellow deplorables and this will surely help us. We'll see how it goes. Either way, we will not be pushed around.

I guess if there's any consolation, if it all goes to hell, at least we'll go down fighting. Amen!

Chapter 2 Democrats Hate America, Trump, & God

This is what HATE looks like!

Democrats don't just hate our President. They hate America!

Many normal Americans and even politicians are waking up and coming to the conclusion that Democrats Hate America. They also hate Trump; and they Hate God.

Rick Saccone, PA-18 GOP nominee spoke up and made comments about his opinion of modern Democrats at one of his campaign rallies. He was a political candidate in the Spring 2008 but failed in both bids.

Besides Saccone, more and more Americans are concluding that the Democrats either hate everything in the world that is not Democrat or they are pretty good fakers.

Saccone made his opinion well-known at a rally at a local volunteer fire department in Blaine Hill, PA. Prior to the early 2018 special election, Saccone is quoted in a video posted to Twitter by NBC News saying:

Isn't this a perfect way to show Democrat disregard for Americans

"They say the other side is energized. Let me tell you; they're energized for hate for our president. They have a hatred for our president. I've talked to so many of these on the left, and they have a hatred for our president. And I tell you, many of them have a hatred for our country... I'll tell you some more—my wife and I saw it again today: They have a hatred for God," Saccone said. "It's amazing. You see it when I'm talking to them. It's disturbing to me."

Mr. Saccone, it is disturbing to me also as well as most America-loving and God-loving Americans. I know the good people of America will make the power-hungry Democrat poor losers pay for that in the next election. All Americans see what is going on.

I am at a loss to be able to say how a Democrat can win any election today by damning God and by damning America. I know many Democrats and the only way they are going for what clearly is bully mob-rule is because they actually don't believe what is in their own faces. I am beginning to think that America would be better off without a Democrat Party.

Need Muscular Conservatism

Conservatives have observed extremely negative and mostly outlandish Democrat behavior for years and have thirsted over those years for a more muscular and unapologetic conservatism and for the bright light of truth to be directed onto these darkest habits of modern leftists.

When the regular people spoke at the ballot box in 2016, the election of Donald Trump began to propel us down a road featuring satisfying helpings of both.

America got to see the full regalia on a stunning day, September 27, 2018. One-time milk-toast Republicans arose in resolve like nothing in recent memory. The accompanying reputational suicide of several key Democrats tied a bow around a historic day for a clarity showing just what these people are and what they stand for.

Almost everybody in the country, friend and foe observed the occasion with shock and alarm. It was not that long ago that the totally unnecessary session of testimony by Supreme Court nominee

Brett Kavanaugh and his main accuser of sexual misbehavior, Dr. Christine Blasey Ford was front and center in the news.

The occasion was needless because Dr. Ford's story in no way rose to the level of credibility to dislodge the nomination. No decent society smears people for life based on high school misbehavior, so even if the wholly unsupported story were true, there would have been a strong argument against its relevancy today.

Nonetheless, there we were, a nation bathed in the splendor of TV screens for a day that began with Dr. Ford's compelling testimony. However, the poised delivery of her story in no way increased its credibility. Only corroborating evidence can do that, and none arose to bolster her claim of a sexual assault at Kavanaugh's hands.

For Kavanaugh's part, he knew he was being railroaded by unscrupulous Democrat Senators as did most of the nation. He sat down with a bolder, more resolved countenance than we saw on his understated Fox News interview.

If we generalize the comments—that the left hates God, they are no truer than the idea that the right, the party that most white evangelicals align with, loves God. Whether it helps politically or not, it is true. More and more brave political candidates are finally seeing the light and making such assertions.

Meanwhile Democrats are busy hating Trump, God, and the United States of America. What do they expect to gain? Replacement voters from south of the border is the only answer. No wonder Democrats fight so hard to undermine America.

Democrats love to hate

In dropping white males from the list of eligibles for the Party, Democrats have come to hate all Americans who love the precepts of the founding. Moreover, they definitely have come to hate God. There is no doubt about that.

Where did all this hate come from? It seems like it is just in the past few years that the odor of hate in America is strong enough (if you'll pardon me) to knock a buzzard off a "sh--" wagon. To use a big word to describe it-- is palpable. The Democrats hate God and because they believe God loves America, they hate America. Everybody knows it but when asked, they have so little regard for the truth, Democrats will deny it.

Can we do anything about it? Well, one thing is for sure, if "we the people" as a group do not smarten up, things will get a lot worse and they may never get better again. A visitor from another planet would quickly recognize that Democrats are the biggest haters of all things in

America. If we could convince them to find another country to destroy, that would be a fine start.

Democrats are so caught up in hating Trump etc., they have no time to work on representing their constituents and so they do not, Consequently, while Donald Trump is making America great again with better paying jobs and the lowest unemployment rate in 50 years, Democrats and the Democrat Party are too busy hating to do any of the people's business in Congress.

They choose instead not to believe all the evidence that Trump is good for America and they do everything they can to stop Trump even when he is doing the will of the people and serving the needs of Democrats and Republicans alike.

Some of us who are vestiges of a once effective Democrat Party would like to see the Party elders begin to love both God and America again. I would suggest they try talking to the Lord Jesus Christ every day for starters if they want their luck to turn.

America has its share of issues for sure, but we are still free to change the country through the election process and of course, we can also start by changing ourselves. Democrats need a changing! According to the founders, it was not supposed to be this way. There is a lot of reason to feel hate today – mostly because there is a lot of hate being thrown at everybody by a lot of Democrats and their sycophantic corrupt media. When do you remember in your lifetime that the press was corrupt. Well, folks, they sure are.

We see no love for regular Americans coming from the mostly miserable, always unhappy media outlets such as the ugly Grey Lady New York Times; MSNBC; and CNN. I used to blame the mainstream media but let's face it, MSNBC, CNN, and the New York Times are responsible for most of the lies and the hate in America today. Let's call it as we see it. They hear the Democrat lies and as if they are true, they publish them. This media is controlled by evil and they have no conscience.

The most recent best thing that has happened to America is that after watching the Democrats dismantle the good in America for years, even during Republican Administrations, God intervened and gave us all another chance. He sent his beloved Son over two thousand years ago and though that helped, just recently, God saw that things do not stay right with mankind for too many years at a time.

This time, to help his intervention, He found a playboy rogue out in the fields of fun and prosperity in America and He let this rogue know that he had a big job for him. Donald Trump, who did not need God's job offer as life was treating him pretty good already, chose to accept the offer and he ran for President of the most powerful country in the world—the US. And, now he is here with us and we better not blow this opportunity to do the right thing for God. Stop the hate!

Poll says Democrats hate America???

It is not an opinion that Democrats hate America. There are actual numbers to prove it. In recent survey one, for example, 81% of Republicans but only 52% of Democrats believe "America is clearly the greatest nation in the world." A Gallup survey showed similar negative Democrat sentiment.

More and more analyses and opinions point to the fact that Democrats hate America. A recent Gallup poll shows only 32 percent of Dems are "extremely proud" to be an American, versus a substantially higher number of Republicans. The low showing on the "extremely proud" scale doesn't immediately translate into "I hate America." But it is getting close to the truth that for too long we all have been observing.

What else can it be? Even if you look at it half-hearted you can see the hate steaming on the sidewalks of America like other matter. How about Antifa anyone? What about Maxine Waters? But any half-hearted political watcher can see that for him- or herself, anyway.

Trump tweeted about Maxine in June 2018 when she was calling for a revolt v all Trump supporters. Trump's Tweet: "Congresswoman Maxine Waters, an extraordinarily low IQ person, has become, together with Nancy Pelosi, the Face of the Democrat Party. She has just called for harm to supporters, of which there are many, of the

Make America Great Again movement. Be careful what you wish for Max!?"

What about Alexandria Ocasio-Cortez and Bernie Sanders, and all the socialists creeping out of their muck piles to swear allegiance to a country they want to substantially change? In the Gallup survey, Republicans came in at 74 percent "extremely proud" to be American, compared to 32 percent of Democrats. In 2016 when Obama led the country, Dems checked in with fully 46 percent extremely proud. I guess Democrats don't like a bustling economy? What else can it be?

Gallop concluded that "Left-leaning groups' antipathy toward Donald Trump and their belief that other countries look unfavorably on the president are likely factors in their decline in patriotism, particularly the sharp drops in the past year." The fact is that the way Democrats are acting, like the crazy train they've been riding, virtually guarantees they're going to face another wave of Republican leadership, another four years of the very White House administration they detest. Can you imagine if Gallup asked "Do you hate America" and posted names?

Ironically, the person sent by God to America to help stop the hate and turn our country into something that as in the days of the founders could be great again, has seemingly caused more hate from poor-loser Democrats than any mere mortal would have ever imagined.

God had to know the hate was coming but he hoped we would all figure out how to contain it and assure that the gift from God himself, Donald J. Trump Jr., would be used to gobble up the hate and help set America on a course to be great again--in both material ways and spiritual ways.

Instead, in addition to hating Trump, the newly caustic, nasty, dirty Democrat Party (sorry, the truth sometimes does not sound good) began to tell working class people, Trump and even God, that they simply did not matter.

Power is the only thing that matters to the Democrat hate machine. God gave the power to Trump so Democrats believe they are obligated to hate God the Father, Son, and Holy Ghost. Oh, yes, there are other reasons why Democrats hate God but Trump is the big one.

Democrats would do themselves well to read this book, since there is only one God and even Democrats have just one soul.

And, yes, Virginia, there is just one Hell also, but it is large enough to fit-in all the hate-mongering Democrats if they choose to continue to waddle in the swill. God would love it, however, if at the end of time, there was a lot of open space in Hades. Stop the hate and make God smile!

Few books are a must-read but another book I wrote titled, *Why Democrats Hate God*, along with this treasure that you are reading, will quickly appear at the top of America's most read list. If we do not gain back the greatness of our America, with the right amount of love v hate, with the help of willing, ahem, God-loving Democrats, somebody may come along one day and have no problem taking this great country and all of its resources away from us all. For starters look at Russia, China, and the Middle East.

To recap with different words, it may sound like an extreme statement to say that Democrats hate America, but really it is not extreme. They are. Moreover, we should not be surprised, for it's been out there for a while now.

Democrats hate America. Other than having the Constitution in their way for converting this country to socialism, and the possibility that the promulgators may get the highest positions in the new order, there are no other reasons why the US should abandon capitalism for socialism. Socialism only works for the big shots left when the proletariat finishes its work. The regulars gain nothing. Three-House Bernie Sanders and the seven + seven Democrat Dwarfs would all be in the new socialist order hierarchy.

All of this socialism crap did not start when Michelle Obama said 'For the first time in my adult life I'm finally proud of my country.' It did not start when Barack called his fellow citizens who opposed him 'bitter clingers,' or when we found out about Barack (& Michelle) Obama's long-time association with Reverend 'God Damn America'

Wright and Screwy Louie Farrakhan would be more important than Obama's relationship with America. The people still believed.

It didn't start when Hillary & Biden attacked not only President Trump but his voters, calling them *deplorables* and *dregs of society* respectively. Nor did it start when the newly crowned socialist princess of the Democrat Party, Sandy, aka Alexandria Ocasio Cortez, said that illegal immigrants 'are acting more in an American tradition' than the President.

No, folks it's always been there with the Left. It's just that they were once smart enough to mask it. In the past their credo dictated that they never got to say it. They knew then that it would cost them politically. Now, Democrats and the sycophant corrupt press simply do not care. They think they rule the people and not vice versa. The Democrats lie and the press swears to it, and the people of all Parties are simply confused until they figure it out. It is not good for America and that ought to be enough for most to know.

So, Democrats have just indulged your patriotism—your plebian belief in God, guns and religion to get your vote, while surreptitiously working to undermine and undo everything that you believe in. But in recent time, they've taken the masks (and the gloves) off, and now they are going full Monty.

Add to that an emboldened new freshman class of far-left radical Socialists, one of whom said 'we're going to impeach the mother-fu**er', and you're going to see not only more division in an already very divided country, but an unapologetically radical, far-left turn by the Democrat Party.

As a registered Democrat myself, I got the message to take the turn with the leaders but I say No way Jose! I love myself and I love my country more than a bunch of nothings who are too willing to destroy my country for their own selfish ambitions. I hope you all look at that is happening honestly and that you make the same decision I have made. God bless you all in these tough times.

Amen!

Chapter 3 Theodore Roosevelt (TR) On America and Immigrants

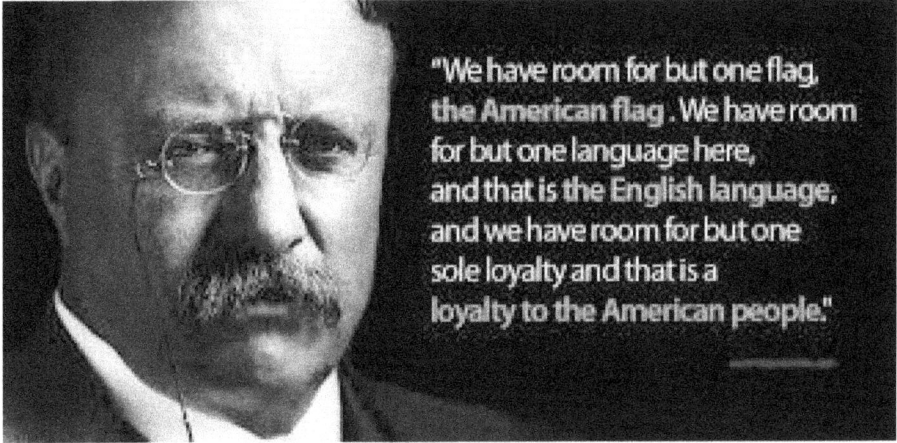

"We have room for but one flag, the American flag . We have room for but one language here, and that is the English language, and we have room for but one sole loyalty and that is a loyalty to the American people."

Would Senator Chuck Schumer today accept Teddy Roosevelt's words?

Schumer is an anti-American with an agenda that does not include Americans. TR was an American who thought as every regular man in America thought at the time. America first! I bet nobody in the world could get Schumer to say: "America first!" Too many others come before US. That's is why Mr. Chuck hates Mr. Trump. The bad guys shudder when they see good guys on the horizon.

There is a well-played quote from Theodore Roosevelt, which expressed his views on immigration and immigrants. Roosevelt felt very similar to regular Americans today about this matter. Of course, back then in the early 1900's it was not such a delicate subject. Popular sentiment was that both Americans and America were not only OK; we were special. It was a necessary fact of life. Roosevelt's posture was quite easy to say and easy to understand.

Roosevelt believed that immigrants should assimilate, become loyal Americans, and speak English. Case closed! Amen! Teddy Roosevelt, often classified as a Progressive, would not like Chuck Schumer or

Nancy Pelosi or any of the anti-Americans trying to bring America down.

Though often attributed to a 1907 speech, these words from then former President Roosevelt were not written until January 3, 1919 in a letter to the President of the American Defense Society. Shortly afterwards, the speech was read publicly at a meeting on January 5, 1919. Roosevelt died the next day, on January 6, 1919. It can be argued that Roosevelt's dying thoughts on official matters were on immigration and its importance to the country.

As most of us know, unlike his more famous fifth cousin Franklin D. Roosevelt, Theodore Roosevelt was the 26th President of the United States

and at the time, the youngest to ever occupy the Oval Office. Ironically, Eleanor Roosevelt, the wife of Franklin D., was TR's niece. TR had been Vice President to President William McKinley when in 1901 McKinley was assassinated. At that time, the young Roosevelt took over at age 42. As an aside, at age 43 President John F. Kennedy was the youngest to ever be *elected* President.

The actual text from Theodore Roosevelt's letter is below:

"We should insist that if the immigrant who comes here does in good faith become an American and assimilates himself to us, he shall be treated on an exact equality with everyone else, for it is an outrage to discriminate against any such man because of creed or birth-place or origin.

"But this is predicated upon the man's becoming in very fact an American and nothing but an American. If he tries to keep segregated with men of his own origin and separated from the rest of America, then he isn't doing his part as an American. There can be no divided allegiance here. . . We have room for but one language here, and that is the English language, for we intend to see that the crucible turns our people out as Americans, of American nationality, and not as dwellers in a polyglot boarding-house; and we have room for but one soul loyalty, and that is loyalty to the American people."

Could President TR have made himself any clearer that America is for Americans, not foreigners. Some other famous Teddy Roosevelt quotes on immigration include the following:

"Every immigrant who comes here should be required within five years to learn English or to leave the country... English should be the only language taught or used in the public schools." Roosevelt gave this statement to the Kansas City Star in 1918.

"We can have no "50-50" allegiance in this country. Either a man is an American and nothing else, or he is not an American at all."

"We cannot afford to continue to use hundreds of thousands of immigrants merely as industrial assets while they remain social outcasts and menaces any more than fifty years ago, we could afford to keep the black man merely as an industrial asset and not as a human being. We cannot afford to build a big industrial plant and herd men and women about it without care for their welfare. We cannot afford to permit squalid overcrowding or the kind of living system which makes impossible the decencies and necessities of life.

We cannot afford the low wage rates and the merely seasonal industries which mean the sacrifice of both individual and family life and morals to the industrial machinery. We cannot afford to leave American mines, munitions plants, and general resources in the hands of alien workmen, alien to America and even likely to be made hostile to America by machinations such as have recently been provided in the case of the two foreign embassies in Washington.

We cannot afford to run the risk of having in time of war men working on our railways or working in our munition plants who would in the name of duty to their own foreign countries bring destruction to us. Recent events have shown us that incitements to sabotage and strikes are in the view of at least two of the great foreign powers of Europe within their definition of neutral practices. What would be done to us in the name of war if these things are done to us in the name of neutrality?"

In his book, On America, TR captures the sentiments of all patriotic Americans:

"The foreign-born population of this country must be an Americanized population - no other kind can fight the battles of America either in war or peace.

"It must talk the language of its native-born fellow-citizens, it must possess American citizenship and American ideals. It must stand firm by its oath of allegiance in word and deed and must show that in very fact it has renounced allegiance to every prince, potentate, or foreign government.

"It must be maintained on an American standard of living so as to prevent labor disturbances in important plants and at critical times. None of these objects can be secured as long as we have immigrant colonies, ghettos, and immigrant sections, and above all they cannot be assured so long as we consider the immigrant only as an industrial asset.

"The immigrant must not be allowed to drift or to be put at the mercy of the exploiter. Our object is not to imitate one of the older racial types, but to maintain a new American type and then to secure loyalty to this type. We cannot secure such loyalty unless we make this a country where men shall feel that they have justice and also where they shall feel that they are required to perform the duties imposed upon them.

"The policy of "Let alone" which we have hitherto pursued is thoroughly vicious from two stand-points. By this policy we have permitted the immigrants, and too often the native-born laborers as well, to suffer injustice. Moreover, by this policy we have failed to impress upon the immigrant and upon the native-born as well that they are expected to do justice as well as to receive justice... that they are expected to be heartily and actively and single-mindedly loyal to the flag no less than to benefit by living under it. "

As a final quote for this book, to set the stage for an America first and Americans first immigration plan, and to help explain how off kilter, the Democrat Press and the Democrat party have become since TR, let's examine this final quote in this book from Theodore Roosevelt:

"The men who do not become Americans and nothing else are hyphenated Americans; and there ought to be no room for them in this country. The man who calls himself an American citizen and who yet shows by his actions that he is primarily the citizen of a foreign land, plays a thoroughly mischievous part in the life of our body politic. He has no place here; and the sooner he returns to the land to which he feels his real heart-allegiance, the better it will be for every good American. There is no such thing as a hyphenated American who is a good American. The only man who is a good American is the man who is an American and nothing else...."

We would do well to include as many of Roosevelt's principles in any plan adopted as any plan should be as Roosevelt would have it: "For Americans First." Donald Trump is a good American, given to the people of the USA by God. That is why he is so detested by the worst of Americans, the corrupt Democrats and their enablers—the corrupt press. The wimpy Republicans stand no better in the eyes of Americans for sure. We hope God opens their eyes and those of the "Never Trumpers."

This chapter does not introduce plans for border walls or for dealing with the problem of 60 million illegal foreign residents in the country today. However, it does set the stage for the rest of this book and how it is more than feasible to one day have an honest immigration plan that benefits Americans more than foreign nationals.

Just as Theodore Roosevelt was a regular and good American, his thoughts and words, not the thoughts and words of faux Americans such as Chuck Schumer, Nancy Pelosi, and the gang of eight tyrants, should be the guiding principles for how we fashion our future comprehensible and sane immigration policies.

Roosevelt did not complain about the laws; he enforced the laws. If our current administration and the administrations before and after Reagan enforced the laws already on the books, perhaps the many 1200-page odyssey bills would not be what the progressive socialists in Congress think we now need. They would already have been expelled from the Congress by the voters.

America in the early twentieth century was not plagued as badly as today by crooked politicians whose selfishness was unabated by a countervailing force. Like President Reagan, and President Trump, President Theodore Roosevelt was a true American and he was the countervailing force against the socialist progressive activists in Europe and in the US.

Moreover, the American people were better schooled on history in Roosevelt's time and they understood its consequences on their lives. They also understood the meaning of tyranny. Therefore, the notion of giving people who had broken US laws a free pass and free lodging and free food was an idea Roosevelt would never believe could happen in his America. Trump is of the same ilk but he needs a better set of advisors that better reflect the will of the people. Of course, an honest Congress with America-First as its credo would also help a great measure.

Nonetheless, in some ways, Roosevelt is chronicled as a progressive himself. But he was not a communist or a leftist socialist radical interested in disrupting the Founders' America. TR's philosophy was a far cry from the progressive-socialists-on-steroids Alinsky-Obama-Clinton-Cortez model of today. In fact, in 1912, TR's Progressive Party ("Bull Moose") ran against Eugene Debs of the Socialist Party.

So, unlike some popular conservatives, one in particular with whom I most often agree, I happen to like TR as a great learner and an honest broker of the truth as he understood it at the time. TR did a lot of good for America, and his thoughts on immigration are about the best I have seen. I think that if TR were alive today, he would be more of a libertarian than a progressive.

TR would be 100% against the gang of eight tyrants' amnesty or any amnesty. He would have said: "Get a job!" If he could have gotten the great group the Silhouettes, to sing the song, it would be sung throughout America. It would have become as patriotic of a theme as "It's a grand ole flag!"

America is for Americans!

Get a Job

Ev'ry morning about this time
She get me out of my bed
A-crying, get a job
After breakfast ev'ry nay
She throws the want ads right my
way
And never fails to say
Get a job, sha na na na, sha na na
na na

And when I get the paper
I read it through and through
And my girl never fails to say
If there is any work for me
And when…

Chapter 4 Who Pays for the Big Bonanzas

What is this all about?

Conservatives like me, love helping all who need help. We are for
America and Americans first! I have always believed in helping the
helpless. My problem is that I don't think government should foster
programs that help make people helpless. Thus, few of US want to
give up our homes, our cars, our bank accounts, or our pensions to
anybody else, period. AOC demands we give them up. I say "No
way!"

Interlopers have a right to take a shot at a better life on a whim.
Nobody can stop them taking a chance. However, just because they
figured out a way to be in America illegally and they have no problem
taking from me or from any of US for their own benefit, does not
mean it is right or that I should like it. We should offer help in their
home country. They should not have to come knocking on our front
door to get help.

I see welfare to illegal immigrants as theft. I say sorry to these folks
since they have just met up with a number of conservative fellows

who do not want to give up another inch of our America! You took a chance, and it is time that you stop costing Americans! Any questions? When you can make it on your own give us a call here in America and tell us what you have to offer our country.

I would advise the interlopers who are remaining undetected to get what they need from the elites in the US, who convinced them originally that it was OK to come. They should get what they need from the US elites who told them they needed no passport, and who convinced them they would have rights that most American citizens do not even have.

Cash, food, medical help, education, and a zillion other necessary things in everybody's life have a cost. To the receiver, who is asked to put nothing into the game, it is a game won, while the losers are those who contribute from their sweat earnings. It is a zero-sum game. Somebody pays when somebody takes. Americans are not giving to charity. Our dollars are being confiscated by our government and given to foreigners living illegally in our country.

In other words, that which somebody takes in America, somebody else gives. There are no free lunches. In April 2013, I wrote a check to the US treasury for a lot of money to pay taxes that I had not expected to owe. Yet, I had to pay anyway. I had already had taxes withheld. Paying these taxes was painful, and so I most certainly care how they are used, and from my point of view they should not be given to an interloper who took a chance that I would be willing to support them. I am not.

Knowing that it will cost over $30,000 per year for each illegal alien in the future, if there are only 10 million in the country should give US all pause. If there are 50 million, the toll on Americans will be the same as if there are 10 million and the cost is $150,000 each. If Warren Buffet and Bill Gates can't dream of paying for all of the freeloading about to happen, how can you or I?

Certain people say it much better than I

Mark Krikorian, who is the director of the non-partisan Center for Immigration Studies, wrote a column for National Review, and he was quite blunt, and even more effective: Listen in your hearts to these words, and if you are like me a bit, you will wish that our Senators were saying them:

"Once the amnesty is safely out of the way, does anyone think Speaker Pelosi and President Clinton III (or President Bush III) won't seek the watering down even of these triggers in order to get people their green cards faster? "Most Americans share Jeff Sessions' and Krikorian's long-held skepticism.

Rasmussen Reports does a good job of nailing down the real opinions out in people-land. In his May 5 - May 6 2013 analysis, the Rasmussen Reports survey said that the people don't believe that the US government would follow through on promises of improved border enforcement. Look at the truth in that as Democrats are not willing to help in any way today to stem the tide of illegal immigration. Because it helps their future voter base, in fact, they prefer no action.

When we consider that Ronald Reagan was duped by promises of enforcement, it all ties into an ages-long promise of correction with no intention by Congress to ever keep the promises they make. We simply cannot trust them.

Chapter 5 American Legislators Have Forgotten for Whom They Work!

Russia once was the propaganda leader

If Communist Russia had as fine a Propaganda Minister as the three mainstream TV networks in America, plus the federal government itself, the USSR would still be the name of a place to live. The Union of Soviet Socialist Republics would still be alive. All the "stans" would be part of the empire and all would be pleased. Well, not exactly! The Socialists would have proven that outside of America, they could survive. But even they know they cannot.

Eventually the lies catch up to you. Mr. Gorbachev turned out to be a good man at a good time and so Russia as the USSR is now merely Russia, and Poland is Poland. The brutal USSR is dead while for the longest time Obama was trying to reincarnate all of the ills of the USSR right here in our own backyard. Illegal foreign nationals that have never lived an American dream may have found cold-war Russian life quite acceptable. Americans would always opt for more.

Americans know in their hearts that our politicians have and continue to deliver to them the proverbial "bad end of the stick." It is what it is. We are handed one lie after another. I have calculated that the estimated total $41 Billion deportation cost from about ten years ago would pay for itself and be a big bargain for taxpayers even if it were lots higher—but we already know that the estimate is way too high. We can afford expulsion if we choose. Only the press and lying Democrats will tell you that we cannot.

Up to 60 million or more illegal foreign nationals

The United States is now occupied by 30 to 60 million more illegal foreign nationals than were in the country for the Reagan amnesty in 1986. (My estimate is 60M.) Worse than that, the CBO says that in the next twenty years, an additional 46 million would have taken up residence illegally if the big gang of eight tyrants' amnesty from 2013 had slipped through the cracks and became law.

If Democrats could be trusted (and they cannot) with keeping their border promises, this would never have happened and it would never happen again. Just like now, Democrats in 1986 promised the border would be secure and impregnable. They did not tell the truth then and they, along with Democrats and the RINOs are not telling the truth now. They claim they want a secure border but are not too keen on the tools needed to keep the border impregnable. How is that?

Neither Republicans nor Democrats ever plan to make the border secure. Get used to it. When you see their lips moving about border security, know they are lying. Washington is the problem, not the solution for illegal immigration. The people who make their living from Washington D.C. Inc. do not think like the real Americans in the real parts of the country.

Those of us who live where the rubber meets the road, and that is not Washington D. C., folks, brought about out own change in 2016—a change bigger than any seen in America, perhaps ever. A man named Trump who keeps his word, disrupted the notion of truth through dishonesty. He was simply honest and he fought with a bunch of dishonest Democrats for the people's concurrence to build a border wall to keep America safe. Americans signed up in droves and elected him president.

Democrats are more interested in more D voters and they fought the president on the means to control immigration no matter what his plan happened to be. Democrats do not care about the USA. They care only about power and more voters coming from the illegal community. But, then again, you already know that.

Fifty million plus ten plus another 46 million is an awful lot of illegal people from other countries. To put that number in perspective, the legal population of Canada is just 37 million. If all resident illegal foreign nationals were in a separate US state, it would be the most populous state in the nation. The sign that most appropriately captures the notion behind the bulk of the immigration interlopers is captured below:

The sign makes me sad just as it makes you sad. If the sign as presented represented other impoverished countries or the countries from which the colonists came from the 1600's onward, perhaps their apparent free flight, as depicted in the sign, would not be the case. Not everybody is free to jump from their own country to take advantage of the people in another.

Even fewer are free to jump to the country they choose from the grab-bag of possible countries if they succeed in their first jump. America and Americans should not feel eternally resigned to mop-up operations for intrinsically guilty liberal progressives, who would like to help everybody on earth as long as they can charge somebody else for the expense—such as a vulnerable American regular guy.

Liberal progressive Democrat leaders leave the regular American citizens in their party behind when they lobby that illegal aliens should be treated better than Americans. When Democrats declare that illegals should not be deported for any reason and instead should be offered sanctuary when they commit crimes—who does that help? It certainly does not help Americans struggling to survive.

Since American laws from the beginning offer deportation as the only remedy, why is it that with a large federal force of immigration officials in all categories, paid by our government (US), we cannot do better in preserving America for Americans? Let me give you a hint at the answer:

C-O-N-G-R-E-S-S

Congress, especially Democrats in Congress have no problem paying a large force of human beings to protect the border. However, they do have a big problem passing laws that are necessary for these human beings to do their jobs. The asylum problem comes to mind immediately. Of course, to Democrats hurting Trump in some small way is more important than helping America in a big way.

Who was the first official that said America was for non-citizens? Nobody in Washington will admit that but that is their de facto position. The political party of those folks is almost 100% Democrat and the part that is not is about 30% RINO. It is getting tough to be a regular guy in America today—one thinking our government is in business to help Americans. It was once easy.

Liberal progressive Democrat leaders complain regularly that American citizens who have no work and have no chance of work are being nasty when they refer to the influx of illegal foreign nationals into America as an invasion. What else is it? Despite the rhetoric, it is an invasion and nothing less. These Americans love President Trump because his plan places Americans above the illegal interlopers who heretofore have gained the plunder of America without any sweat labor.

The big problem for years, especially in Obamatimes, formerly working Americans, is that illegal foreign nationals unabashedly and unapologetically took all jobs; just as locusts take and eat all edible plants and leave stubble behind in their wake. Yet, rather than condemn these foreign invaders, our government officials, from President Obama on down, applauded the foreigners for having left some stubble behind for Americans to enjoy.

Progressive leaders believe that labeling illegal aliens as invaders is inaccurate and insulting and these leaders do not want to hurt the feelings of any interlopers. It has been apparently OK, however, to hurt the feelings and the livelihood of Americans in this process of making foreign invaders feel good. My President, Donald J. Trump and I are on a trek to make Americans feel good about being Americans.

Is it really OK that Americans pay the freight for the many illegal foreign nationals who are able to trick the system into gaining benefits, such as education for their children, medical help, and even food and cash? And, is it really OK if you are a liberal progressive Democrat, for millions of regular Americans to lose their jobs rather than have you and your ilk attempt to enforce border protections that are built into US immigration law? If Democrat big shots think Democrats should fund illegal aliens, let them be the first to throw their wallets into the pool.

When an illegal is not captured at the border, or is in the visa overstay category, it is even more amazing that our government (Obama regime especially) chose to let the interlopers take American jobs rather than deport them. This is against our Constitution. Washington lies and tells us we cannot afford to deport them all. Just the opposite is the truth. We cannot afford to feed, support and nurse them well. Democrats are hoping that if the illegal aliens of today are given a vote in national elections, there will no longer be a Constitution. They plan the overthrow of America in the Ocasio Cortez Congress. She and her buddies have no use for "Americans."

Has America been invaded?

The Webster dictionary people are an excellent source to find the meaning of words. Let's ask them if we have been invaded or not. We know that American citizens have not crossed our southern border to invade and plunder Mexico or any of the South American countries. However, we cannot say the same for those foreign nationals that have illegally entered our country from the south.

The Webster definition of an invasion is simply "any entry into an area not previously occupied." This definition proves the term "invasion" is accurate. As for insulting, besides not wanting illegal foreign nationals to be referred to as invaders, progressives are so caught up in the PC world that they argue that they should not be referred to as "illegal aliens" either.

Yet, in code for the US immigration law, that is the term the writers used. Crooked politicians, mostly Democrat, unfortunately as I am a registered Democrat, like to redefine terms for their own use and they like to rewrite history when it is convenient for them.

So much for insulting the illegal foreign nationals! Unless we choose not to use our language properly, the illegal foreign nationals residing in the US are both illegal aliens plus invaders. They are foreign nationals because they have allegiance to a foreign country, not to America. Their children, who have not been born in the US, have the same status.

Why can we not call things what they are? Simply because somebody's agenda prohibits it, and the US press is corrupt and their game is to play against regular Americans. Our liberal progressive legislators are comfortable treating illegal foreign nationals better than US citizens from the moment that they escape from border guards, and they move next door to you. BTW, they never can get in the gated communities of our legislators so Congress never sees first-hand the havoc which they wreak upon the people.

Right after they break into (invade) our country, or the moment they choose not to go home when their visas expire, our progressive legislators have the welcome signs ready. In 2013, Marco Rubio and all of the Democrat and RINO members of the gang of eight "tyrants"—sought to preserve a fine way of life for these non-Americans at our expense.

Liberal progressive Democrats had hoped that citizens would not notice the presence of so many people in America that cannot speak English. They even have introduced other languages in our schools so that we think it is natural to speak multiple languages in America. Just because illegal foreign nationals are in every city in the US, as Hillary Clinton would say: "What difference should that make?"

Hispanics and Latinos are not the only foreign nationals in the US

Fat chance they would be noticed! There are massive numbers of illegal Irish in New York for sure. Haven't you noticed? The gang of eight must have gotten wind that because of whiskey, the Irish are destined to rule the world, and John Jameson may be called back to lead the new empire.

In the greatest act of tokenism since the subway began to take tokens instead of cash, trying to attract a few Irish to their side, the gang of eight tyrants' 1000 plus page proposal also called for 10,500 visas for Irish immigrants, as long as they have the equivalent of a high school degree, and at the time of registration have no obvious whiffs on their breaths.

Yet, there are no such criteria for illegals or as they are now known, "migrants," even if they bring Measles, Chicken Pox, Polio, Tuberculosis, or other deadly diseases with them. Why is this?

Congress can hide behind its gated community barrier while refusing the US a gated entrance. Congress takes more income from those who are not happy with US law than those of us that elect them to do our bidding.

Most Americans do not know that there are forty percent non-Hispanic / non-Latino foreign nationals in the US. Irish and Chinese would fall in on that side of the mix. Most Americans consider what is happening with immigration to be an issue brought on only by Mexico and South America. Not true! America is a ripe place for invasion from all countries wishing to unload its citizens.

Clearly proximity of the interloper country has created most of the problem but 40% is a large "other" number. Many of this 40% have spent a lot of money on transportation and have come a long way to get here. A goodly percentage of this 40% are surely terrorists waiting for another opportunity such as Boston's Tsarnaevs to spring a big surprise on the oppressive American people.

Whoever is here illegally, it is because they have either entered illegally or they have overstayed their visas. Regardless of what the liberal progressive Democrats think or want you to believe, their presence in this country is rightfully termed an "invasion." Were these millions invited by your family or mine? Of course not! They broke in! This is the source of the collective angst of 90% of US citizens who feel discomfort because illegal residents have become OK in our government's eyes. They are not OK in the eyes of American citizens, yet Washington is not listening to US. The government is not performing its sworn duties to uphold the law.

There are very few Americans who are against a reasonable amount of legal immigration, with no preference for race, nationality or ethnicity. But most Americans are against any amount of illegal immigration, regardless of race, nationality or ethnicity.

So, why are there so many illegal foreign nationals dwelling and working in this country if it is not something the American people desire? They were not invited by the American people. However, it can be argued persuasively that they were invited here by lax US government immigration policies, greedy business owners, and a particular political party that thinks if they ever were made citizens, that party would rule the country through the next millennium.

Oh, the name of that party is the Democratic Party and at this moment in time, I am a member of that party and have been since I switched from Independent when I was 23 years old. I joined the Democrat Party when the Democrats not only said they represented ordinary Americans, they actually did represent ordinary Americans. They really were for the working man—the regular Joe on the street.

By the way Republicans are with the Democrats on this scam against Americans. Our politicians on both sides want something from immigration that enriches their private coffers and hurts their constituents. The sooner we all come to grips with the reality that Congress and the President do not want to secure our borders because the alternative makes them and their backers richer, and the money is how they get reelected, the sooner we can get rid of them all. If we the voters ignored their lies in TV ads and the like, they would again do our bidding. Do we have the guts not to reelect these swine? I sure hope so!

Like sheep, the Democratic Party lost its way

It would be a simple solution to just find a shepherd. Over time, the Democrats, my party, lost their way. I have been hanging on, hoping some sense comes to my party of over forty years. Over time, the Party decided that some Marxist-style redistributive welfare-oriented ideology was what they were all about. Ask all the D candidates for office in 2019 and of course the infamous Ocasio-Cortez. I do not know how this party of elite wimps was able to convince all the tough Democrats from lumberjacks to coal miners that I met in my life to surrender themselves to such pitiful governance.

Today's Democrats are interested in keeping the regular American down, while elevating others (foreigners) to their strata using our tax money.

Most Democrats find the change of ideology for the party to have created a bad taste in their mouths but their historical political lineage keeps them in line since they have not yet begun to think about what it really means to them and their families, and the next generation of Americans. By not addressing this with our corrupt leaders, we are making life in America impossible for our offspring. Shame on US!

I believe that I can be a registered Democrat and still be conservative in my views but Democratic leaders would be pleased if I moved on, even if I changed parties. I am sure that if the Democrats had excommunicative powers, such as the Catholic Church, I would be one of the first they would discharge from their Party.

Over the last forty years, the government of the US has been hijacked by progressive liberal socialists. The existing state of affairs on immigration is something they very much desire. And, yes, George Bush, though a Republican was both a progressive and a business owner. His decisions when president, regarding illegal foreign nationals, clearly reflected that posture.

Bush was happy to legalize 'em all. He tried but did not succeed. Nobody really gains with the US labor force working for historically low wages. Bringing in more foreigners to take more jobs has not been the solution.

Bush was not a favorite of mine but I did vote for him twice because Democrats have become the anti-American Party and Bush was better than the alternative. Americans today are fighting both the progressives in Washington, and the businesses in Corporate America, to return the United States back to American citizens. None of the powerful and none of the elites want regular Joes to have any say in government. Before Trump, they were winning.

There is no press or media out there leading the charge for an honest America. Fox News, though more helpful than hurtful, is missing most of the time on the subtleties of the progressive takeover. Fox is a Republican station, not a conservative station. Rush Limbaugh is today's greatest American hero. He actually is our only hope on the air waves. Thank you Rush!

Unfortunately, the corrupt press has done a job on him and weak-kneed Democrats who choose not to think for themselves have bought the gibberish about El Rushbo. Regardless, he is the voice of reason in a political world of unreasonable voices.

Illegal Aliens think they are here to stay!

Unfortunately for Americans, the horses are clearly out of the barn and the Illegal aliens of today do not appear like they intend to go back to their home countries any time soon. Who can blame them with such a deal continually on the table from sucker Americans? Why does our Congress permit this? Easy answer, somebody is paying them for feeling so good about being anti-American. Don't doubt me please or you will find you are wrong.

One of the unmentioned facts about illegal aliens of today compared to those of yesteryear, is they don't even look for short-term permissions. They don't ever intend to go back. One could create an effective argument that postures the following—rather than retreat, they plan to bring so many new people into the country that the new people will take over America and leave traditional Americans far behind. Will they be as kind to US as we have been to them? Think hard about that as Americans become the minority in America!

Irish seem to assimilate but I cannot know for sure since it has been at least one century for my family to have done what was necessary to become citizens. The new breed of immigrants is more like the early Chinese who built the railroads almost single handedly. They were devoted to being part of their own life, independent of that of Americans.

The new illegal alien is not interested in the old-time melting pot or the idea of assimilation. In fact, they would prefer that the national language of the US be changed to Spanish or Chinese or perhaps even Gaelic. Unlike times past, these folks are more prepared to overtake Americans in America, rather than assimilate. Judge this statement from their sheer numbers and their anti-American demonstrations.

Chapter 6 A Congress Full of Wimps & Cowards

Wimps & Cowards in the Flesh

Congress makes it all worse by design

It is too bad that we Americans need the Congress to solve problems as they always seem to have more important things to do.

Cowardly Democrats and Republicans alike in Congress are the bane of the American people. It would be tough to find a greedier, more corrupt lot in any government anywhere. They are nothing like the founders. They continue to exist because people are too trusting.

Congress is slick and uncaring and they know how to accumulate personal wealth while in office. Check it out. US citizens are like babes in the woods to be trampled on by these self-serving narcissists.

Don't expect anything from your representatives in either chamber. They no longer believe they need the people. They are intentionally killing government of the people, for the people, and by the people and they are using the good will of the people for their self-serving gains. This must stop.

Of course, time is long overdue for voters to bring out the big cleansing broom from where the founders placed it and sweep this pox on America out of the sacred halls of the Congress once and for all.

Both parties at one time in the course of their election campaigns lied to their respective constituencies. Republicans claimed to advocate nationalistic and conservative policies and Democrats claimed to use a liberal progressive agenda to help the people overcome what they called the big-business mentality of the Republicans. Those days are long gone. Both parties now show disdain in the treatment of their constituents. Democrats, my Party, are worse than Republicans.

I am a registered Democrat who loves America. Democrats no longer permit a love for America. For years I watched Republicans promise the policies which I advocate and then go ahead and join the Democrats in undermining the country. Today, the Democrats take extreme positions on socialism v capitalism, infanticide, border security and taking care of America and Americans first. Americans simply do not count.

If you are a traditionally good American, with Alexandria Ocasio Cortez now serving as the de-facto leader of the Democrat Party which Nancy Pelosi gave to her, you have reason to fear. Democrats no longer lie about their designs on bringing down America; they brag about it openly.

As an example, on Mayday, 2017, the Republican Party showed that the will of regular people in the party of the elephant no longer mattered. Republican elite leadership once again turned over the control of the budget to the wily Democrats. Hard as it is to believe, the truth is more difficult to assimilate than the fake news. Anti-leftists, conservatives, nationalists, populists and regular Americans for America, who might very well be described simply as Trump voters and loyalists, learned a bitter lesson again watching Republican Party leaders give it up for the opposition party. Democrats do not complain to each other about what happened to their party but they do whisper it to themselves. They are afraid to speak up as the Dems will not permit honest discourse.

Conservatives thought Republicans were the answer but they are bigger cowards than Democrats. So, rank and file conservatives still need a representative party that we can count on. That representation has not been delivered by the weak-kneed, elitist establishment Republican leadership.

In the first budget submission of the Trump Administration, for example, Paul Ryan, once a fair-haired boy for all conservatives, and the rest of the Republican Wimps found our backs and stabbed us again. If these cowards could hurt us anonymously, they would, but today, we can recognize them by their limps. It seems both Democrats and Republicans today are limping cowards pushing their own agendas above the people's needs. They both love illegal immigrants. One side of the aisle likes cheap labor and the other likes that the border floodgates deliver Democrat voters.

Values are no longer important to the cowards in Congress. Democrats simply do not care to truly represent the people and conservatives now recognize the one-time Party of Lincoln as frauds that need no longer appear to be important to everyday John Does.

Americans, both Democrats and Republicans who united in 2016 believed that together we had thrown out the swamp with Donald Trump's election. Yet, neither party, especially the elite establishment Republicans ever got the message.

The promised border wall and border security is the most egregious example. Republicans are still afraid of Democrats to do what they promised the voters, while Democrats, other than Ocasio Cortez are deathly afraid of wild-eyed Nancy Pelosi, for fear they will be cut off from the Party's goody bags. Americans have to send all of these fraidy-cats packing.
This cowardly Congress is all-too-real. It might as well be absent all the time as it expends little to no energy on behalf of the people.

Republicans were afraid of a black backlash supposedly and were obviously AWOL during the entire Obama presidency. Then when they had the reins of power, we quickly learned when the Party of

Lincoln submitted its Mayday Budget in 2017 that this cowardly Party's plan was to remain AWOL.

Democrats have been AWOL for an awful long time in terms of their duties to American citizens. Now like Patsy Cline could sing about, they are simply crazy. In other words, it is even worse now that this cowardly Party has gone nuts.

As a Democrat, like many Democrats, I saw the Party leave me. I did not have to leave the Democrat Party. I am convinced that if the Republicans changed the name of their party to The American Party or to the John Doe Party and they got rid of the elite swamp rats, Democrats would join in droves and make the new party unbeatable and unafraid. Right now, there is no good home for misplaced, unrepresented Democrats who vote for Trump. Heck, they have a hard time finding former friends with whom they can have a friendly conversation. You know I am not kidding.

Once thought to be honest to a fault, the Republicans have taken to lying as a tool to survive. But rather than lying to Democrats to snooker them, they lie to their own people, the conservatives, pretending to represent them. With all the Democrat lies about President Trump, the halls of Congress are a veritable lying chamber, and of course the corrupt, liberal, progressive press lies to make sure the people continue to believe that the Democrat darlings in Congress are telling the truth.

Democrat lies seem true. They are the masters of prevarication as telling the truth will destroy their Party. They lie, and the press swears to their lies. However, as neophytes in the lying game, Republicans simply are not as good as Democrats, and they do not have the corrupt press available to back up everything they say.

Republicans chose a while ago to no longer care about the needs of any in the Republican Party other than the fat-cat donors and the K-street lobbyists, and of course the Party elites. They blamed conservatives for losing the Presidency in 2012, yet it was the Republican Party who backed an elite Republican not the anti-leftist conservatives, nationalists, populists, or regular Americans, who caused the defeat.

Though Mitt Romney was not a bad guy in 2012, he is a real self-serving jerk today. I thought he may have made an OK president, but he was not a good candidate for regular Americans, and he did not attract the masses of John Does to the Republican Party. With his crybaby reaction to the Trump Presidency, I would almost prefer a lying Democrat to one of the worst conservatives on record. I hope he decides to be a good Senator for the conservative cause but I no longer trust him.

It really does not matter at this point as it is almost a certainty that Republicans for some time now have been looking for a new constituent base. Anti-leftist, non-elites without huge checkbook balances for the Republican Party today are passé. Wildly dreaming Republicans were hoping that Hispanics would become their new base, and Paul Ryan was commissioned by Republican swamp dwellers to roll regular John Does off a cliff along with Granny.

While Republicans planned the demise of the little guys in the Party, Americans who love America decided to launch a preemptive strike on the elite Republican establishment. We looked for and found a candidate that the wimpy RINO establishment Republicans did not want and surely did not like. We found a smart businessman who did not spend all his life as a suck-up politician.

That man of course is Donald Trump. He is now our President. His election shows that the people can do anything we choose, when motivated. It also shows the people can leave both the Democrat and Republican Party and can do well for ourselves. How about a new Party called The John Doe Party?

Besides talking about the demise of the Congress into a bunch of fraidy-cats, by picking on the cowardly ways of Republicans and Democrats, this book focuses more on Democrats who today have no saving graces and no saving values. They are the worst. While regular Americans such as anti-leftists, conservatives, nationalists, populists, independents, and regular American John Does who love America are leaving the Republican Party leadership, there is no real home yet for us all. Perhaps soon there will be a real John Doe Party.

Conservatives would like a nice spot to move so we can fully pull out of the Republican Party. The Republicans have left us behind and they are not looking back to see if we are following. They don't care because the leadership may very well prefer to be Democrats. Even regular John Doe Democrats would be welcomed in The John Doe Party or perhaps The American Party and so all the John Does in America have a place to go but as of yet, it does not have a name. But, it will!

The good ole boy elite establishment Republicans can learn to swim in their own complacency. America-lovers, conservatives and former Tea Party people, who most often are one and the same, for eight years had a real enemy in the White House. His name as we well know is Barack Hussein Obama, and he had appointed his heir to be Hillary Rodham Clinton. Of course, we the people from two parties not stuck in the swamp did not want that, and so we made Donald Trump—who was the richest regular guy in the country—we made him the President of all America and we are so glad we did.

Why is this book about the worst Democrat leadership ever? Democrats are always the clear and present danger to democracy. The answer hit me like a ton of bricks. It was a wake-up call. What seemed like out of nowhere, the GOP began to stop engaging Democrats as an opposition party by choosing not to help regular Americans in the eight BT (before Trump) years.

The whiny wimpy jawboning Republicans chose not to fight Obama's many anti-American policies. Worse than that, with Trump's ascendancy to the presidency, the Republican RINOs continued to favor Democrats over the anti-leftists John Does that had always supported the Party of Lincoln. By those who believe in God, Trump, not the most religious or the least religious but a guy loaded with redemption, is today looked upon as a Prophet of sorts sent by God in answer to the prayers of Democrat regulars and Republican regulars alike. The other names for Never-Trumpers in modern culture, suffice it to say include the groups Pharisees and Sadducees. Go ahead try to prove me wrong. I love God and I love Trump as a Prophet from the Lord. Despite his irregular demeanor, who else could do what he does?

It seemed like a bad dream when Republicans began to either believe they were dealt a winning hand in the Obama game or they were actually afraid of the President. Either way, these were scary times for Americans. No reinforcements came to the aid of Americans from the Republican Party, which had simply capitulated.

Republican elites would give Democrats whatever they wanted even after winning the Congress. How disappointing. For nine months the Republican *Never-Trumpers* played Congress like as if Trump were guilty of "collusion," and they seemed to figure that he would be gone by the end of 2017. So, these woeful creeps did nothing to help the people who got them elected. Now we all know the Mueller Report was a witch hunt and a political hoax on the American people. When it was unknown, Congress betrayed the President.

There would be no border issue today if in January 2017, Republicans had done the job for which the people elected them. They gave Trump virtually nothing and the border and the wall were not even on their radar other than to say, "NYET!". Republicans paid the price for their cowardice in the midterm elections in 2018. The people need to knock a bunch more of them out of the park in the Spring of 2020. For their crazy behavior, I find no reason for any Democrat in Congress to be reelected

The people saw the resistance his own Party gave to the President's agenda and those not on the Trump wave, paid the price by having to go back and live at home. All in all, with a new socialist Democratic-controlled House, and with Pelosi back in power as their leader, the American people had their retribution but now we are all paying our own price for speaking up and cleaning out a bunch of RINOs. We did the right thing but Democrat cowards will not give us anything in return. They hate America first.

In races across the country, from Virginia to Alabama to South Carolina, the political careers of Trump haters begun to crumble to dust in the elections. Life was a lot better for those who had atoned for blaspheming the President but not enough atoned to save the Republican majority in the House.

There is irony as we all know Democrats are Bad! Bad! Bad! Yet, Regular Americans have gotten accustomed to getting nothing from Republicans. We are sick of it. We have been trained by experience to expect excrement from Democrats and we get it always but we had hope in Republicans for too many years. The Party of Lincoln forgot about their supporters and they forgot about Lincoln. They made a conscious decision not to support the people. Instead they looked only to their donors.

They will do it again unless we send them weeping and gnashing in a new valley of tears. We, those who God charged up to get Trump elected must be prepared to go it alone. When Donald Trump showed up, we knew we had our leader; now we must fight to gain real representation. We must continue the Republican purge by beating the Swamp rats in the primaries. We cannot afford to turn America over to the Democrats.

For years, Americans believed that the Republican Party's values and our values were the same. Regular Americans have not had our own Party, and so for many years or so it seemed, Republicans were the enforcers for our values. Therefore, we logically believed that Republicans felt the same about important matters as we do. We were wrong.

Republicans idiotically made their love affairs with the donor class and the K-street lobbyists well known and began to oppose regular Americans in important life and values matters. With Trump in office, they made it worse, they began to align with the opposition party—i.e. the Democrats. When you find them in the confessional, it is easy to find that few Americans are for the nasty stuff the Democrats are selling. The Green New Deal is full of democrat socialist puffery which is a nicer name for lies.

In both economic and foreign affairs, conservatives watched Obama spend his eight years in an anti-American role. During this time. The cowardly Republicans were like mice afraid to speak. The Republican leadership has been marking time waiting for something supposedly, choosing not to oppose the Democrats. What a bunch of goofs to not oppose the Party you were elected to oppose. It is time for all Americans to oppose all those who think in such convoluted ways.

Republicans became the great pretenders bluffing us that "our day would come," without any pushback to the Obama agenda. Democrats told the truth but their truth was evil. Trump is our honest answer finally. The taste of Democrat rule in just the three first months of 2019 is enough to teach us all that we pay a price when we get rid of RINOS so let's get back some good guys in the 2020 primaries.

That's why this book and others like it are so necessary today. Read folks! Read! We unabashedly recommend that Americans stop trusting Republican hand-shakers and Democrat socialists. Republicans have proven that they will not fight for America or for American values. Democrats now live someplace off the wall where few sane people even visit.

Republican greed unfortunately has trumped the needs of America. The leaders of the Grand Old Party have not even acknowledged that Obama and the Democrats were wrong. Anti-leftist regular Americans such as you and I must learn to go it along. Bye Bye to Republican elites! While we feel this way, we cannot punish the half-ok people by voting in no-OK people—ie—the Democrats or as the cynics call them the Demo-Rats.

The sooner all Americans can cast off Republicans as our only protection against Democrats and progressivism, the sooner we can move on to solving the problem for our values, our country, and our freedom. We need our own Party for sure; for without a Party, Regular John Doe Americans will not even be permitted to help on the battlefield when America is hanging by just a thread.

While we have been waiting for the right time to form a party, most of us think that we can defeat the Democrat leadership, the corporations, the unions, the media, and the traitorous Republicans who are not worth the ground they stand on. The time for waiting is over. It is now time to act.

As a great start, in 2016, Americans from all political backgrounds chose to support Trump as our President. What a great move. He is governing as a good Republican from the olden days, and as a nationalist and conservative working to make America great.

I hope he does not get too frustrated with the anti-Trump power brokers in the GOP. I hope he finds that he can rally the troops such as us, without the Republican Party umbrella. We must stand ready to do our part within a new Party, even if we exist as a clandestine wing of the Republican Party. Our best bet of course is to form our own John Doe Party and get rid of the swamp donors and the Never Trumpers. Our motto can well be that we are the Never Demmers.

Being Democrat is the worst scourge of all.

Yes, we must work together to create a place for regular John Doe Americans—the little guys in America. We must leave the elite establishment to run their own Parties.

Meanwhile, a good Party such as The John Doe Party can take all the regulars in America, including the regular Joe Doe Democrats, John Doe Independents and John Doe members of other Parties who love America. We can do it. Our first step was to get Trump elected and we did that. We the people can do anything. Now that we are motivated, it is time to move forward.

Your author Brian W. Kelly takes nothing for granted. For years and years, he has monitored what is happening to regular Americans and has written extensively on this major problem with the Republican Party. Democrats as we know are even worse, according to Kelly and those of us who have seen the new radical anti-capitalist, infanticide advocating Anti-American cowardly Democrats. We all know Kelly is right.

Brian Kelly is one of America's most outspoken and eloquent conservative speakers and authors on American values. He is the author of 196 books including this one as well as *Saving America the Trump Way; Why Trump?; Taxation without Representation; Obama's Seven Deadly Sins; Kill the EPA!; Jobs! Jobs! Jobs!;* and many other fine patriotic books.

All Kelly books are now available at Amazon, and Kindle. Many can be found at Barnes & Noble and other fine booksellers. Brian's author central link is www.amazon.com/author/brianwkelly.

Like most of you, your author, Brian Kelly is fed up with a stifling progressive liberal agenda in Washington that places the needs of everybody else in front of the needs of Americans. Like many regular John Does, he is shocked at the behavior of the new RINO Republican Party. He is not shocked at the Democrats, however, as a democrat, he saw them swiftly leave the principles of his father and of Thomas Jefferson.

Like you, Kelly is frustrated with how Congress continually tries to deceive us so that we will believe they are still with US on values and policy. They want our votes; but they no longer want to know what we think. It does not matter to the establishment elites in both Parties.

Brian Kelly has read the intelligence reports, has researched and has written about these important topics for years, and he knows how intolerable the results of poor government policy can be within our neighborhoods. His comprehensible and sane recommendations in this book are explained in detail within the covers of this soon-to-be classic offering. *Democrat Secret for Power & Winning Elections* demonstrates that the Democrat Party is filled with so many low-life Representatives it can be cited as a national shame.

It's Time for a big change. It's time for bad representatives to remain buried under big rocks.

This book is part of a new conservative bible to get us back on track with America. It shows why sucking up to Democrats and RINO Republicans is bad for Americans. Kelly tells us all what to do about it. You are going to love this book since it is designed by an American for Americans. Few books are a must-read, but *Democrat Secret for Power & Winning Elections* has all the prospects of ending the party of elites paid for by the US taxpayers.

Thanks to you, *Democrat Secret for Power & Winning Elections* is about to appear at the top of America's most read list. Brian appreciates each book that exits the shelves. Thanks again!

Chapter 7 We Get the Government We Deserve

Do they work for somebody else?

The chasm between electors and the elected is widening as we speak. The John Does and the Jane Q. Publics have lost faith in their representatives. Many have become fully disinterested in the political process, though the healthcare "debate" and the fresh air at the "Town Meetings" may be just the cure for this malaise.

For some time, with good reason, the public has felt disenfranchised from the basic right of a citizen to participate in their democracy. Some may handle this by ignoring politics. Others may find alternative ways to attempt to influence the course of events, sometimes through friends and associates, but not always with very positive results.

Sometimes as we have seen in our history, the frustration of humans in our democracy leads to violence as in the civil rights movements and the anti-war rallies of the 1960's and the riots in Los Angeles in the 1990's. Are we there again? Perhaps the main reason that the system even seems to work is that constituents do not make many demands -- at least till now, and like Reppe says,

"We Get The Government We Deserve. "

This is the root cause that permits politicians, masquerading as our representatives, to represent others' interests. It is an understatement to suggest that representatives are out of touch with the will of the people. Even the newly elected begin to share the wealth of their constituency with others as they begin their "service." They have this need to redistribute income and since 2010 with Obamacare, they have been redistributing healthcare.

This is a common malady of the often elected and the newly elected. They are quickly infected by their "stalwart peers" in the chambers. For a politician, it's "catchier" than the Swine Flu. Elected "representatives" have no problem taking your money and buying votes with it -- even if there is nothing left in the treasury.

Until they got caught by John Q., how many of the "honorables" voted originally to have the non-working and the illegal aliens receive the tax rebate of 2008? The Dems are preparing to provide illegals with social security benefits. That ought to bring in a few more votes.

This trick is like buying future votes, but the motivation is the same. It is never really intended for the downtrodden, hapless, illegal foreign national struggling to make ends meet. Not a chance. It is to puff up the elected to demonstrate their magnanimity and vote-worthiness. The Congress still is getting away with this caper. After all, they make the laws and the bad ones do not apply to them.

Besides your money, they will also take your means of earning a living if it serves their purposes. To please their corporate sponsors, they have no problem taking your job and giving it to a foreign national, either here in the U.S. or in the worker's home country, in China or India. They have just one mission and it is accomplished if they get elected again. The next term of office, not the current one, is all that matters. We get the government we deserve.

The House of Lords

Senators are above it all. They breathe the rarified air reserved for the Gods. If you see a Senator in person once in your life, it is a memorable event. Perhaps you are among the lucky. Perhaps not! Senators have so many people to represent that they operate as Lords, clearly of the nobility (though nobility is expressly forbidden by the Constitution), and they have no need to ever mingle with the common folk. They can't anyway.

In Pennsylvania, for example, the state in which I live, it is the 6th most populated state in the U.S. with an estimated population of 12,500,000. That means that between the two senators, each gets to work with over six million people. No way no how! The Senators know they do not have to represent the people and, so they represent whoever they choose and they still get sent back every six years like it is an entitlement. A sure thing. We get the government we deserve.

The House of Commons

What about our representatives in the House? Why don't we ever see them? Remember that our Constitution clearly specifies the number of senators and representatives. The ratio is fixed at 1 representative for each 30,000 in the electorate. Now, that is still a high ratio but it is workable.

Regardless of what is in the Constitution, however, in the year 1911, the representatives themselves decided to break this basic tenet of the Constitution by adopting a new law. Now, only 435 maximum seats are allocated regardless of the population. This of course has made them all more important and thus worthy of a large salary and expenses. In 2009, for example without unvouchered expenses, your congressman pocketed $174,000.00. Not bad for a part time job. In 2019, the salary is the same because it is not popular with the folks at home for Congress to raise its salary.

With a growing population, the ratio in the House of Representatives right now is about 1 in 700,000. That's an awful lot of hands to shake for just one person. So, they don't, and they know they do not have to shake anybody's hands or meet anybody. And, you don't miss them. But, you should! We get the government we deserve.

If you are good at math, you'll be able to tell this puzzle isn't over yet. Take the twenty-some mostly permanent staff members for each of the 435 representatives and multiply that (about 22) by 435 and add that to the 435 representatives. The number approaches 10,000. With the approximate U.S. citizen population just over 300,000,000 (technically illegal aliens have no representation), it can be argued that the ratio of 1 to 30,000 has magically been maintained, if you're happy talking to an aide instead of your representative.

Why they need 22 or 23 staff members is an enigma I will let hang for another day. The point is that we actually need about 9500 more Congressional Representatives to comply with the Constitution. That would certainly make our representatives much more accountable and maybe we would actually be able to reach them and maybe they would even live in our communities instead of behind gates in secret communities.

And, of course they would not be so "important and honorable," which would be good for the people. It would be a bummer for the Congressman, however, not being quite as important, but so what? Remember, we get the government we deserve.

There are lots of other sound arguments for this notion postured at the Jacksonian party blog at:

http://thejacksonianparty.spaces.live.com/blog/cns!3E751362FDD59519!143.entry

Our benign oligarchy can use a dose of direct democracy

You may choose to read more about the forms of government in the Civics Lesson available across the Internet. Civics is like a vestigial organ such as the Appendix as it is rarely taught any more. We need it for sure as the young get out of school not knowing about the government which they must eventually vote for or against.

You would learn why our form of government is known as a representative constitutional democracy. Instead of every person having a say in every decision, we elect representatives and we hold them accountable through the Constitution to make sure they don't hijack the government.

When a government is of the rich, for the rich, and by the rich, we would call that an oligarchy--rule by the few over the many. Substitute special interests for "rich," and it means the same. As long as we get no representation from our elected, we really do not have a functioning representative democracy. In practice it is an oligarchy and this is very dangerous.

As long as the oligarchy is benign, there is not much reason to be concerned other than that long before the year 2000, the government was already hijacked and still nobody is calling anybody on it. The great insights of Dr. Michael Savage, a well-known syndicated Radio Talk Show Host suggest that the time to get really worried about your free speech is when the few begin sending out the big black cars and one at a time, the many begin to disappear into the gulags.

Back when the big issues began in 2010, it seemed as if the Obama Czars all came equipped with questionable integrity and a tailor-made government hijacking kit. Watch out. We elected Trump to remove the czars. Are they gone? We get the government we deserve.

In a Direct Democracy, the people have the vote, not the representatives, and this type of democracy is based on the principles of Initiation, Referendum, and Recall. Many of the states of the union also have these notions in their constitutions, but our founding fathers believed at the time that the checks and balances they built into the early government would permit the constitutional democracy (Republic) to last for quite a long time.

They originally thought that professionals, such as our senators, originally just one from each state, would be the proper way to run the country. As the Articles of Confederation were woven into the Constitution, this notion changed to two senators per state, not elected directly by the people but by the state legislatures, and a House of Representatives of the people, elected directly by the people.

Checks and balances aren't working

As they say at realdemocracy.com, "DEMOCRACY WON'T WORK UNLESS YOU FIND THE TRUTH AND KEEP YOURSELF INFORMED." Stay ignorant of how things really are and you will almost certainly reap the government you deserve.

The checks and balances of the Founding Fathers include (1) the Constitution itself, and (2) the three "equal" branches of government. But the big trick they had up their sleeves was that the (3) representatives in the House were elected, not appointed and there was a huge electorate to make sure that bad representatives would not be reelected.

In other words, the founders believed that the American people would weed out the bad guys so that the bad guys could not corrupt the government. These three notions were intended to keep the representatives of the government serving the people and not serving special interests. If this were the case in practice, however, I would not have been challenged to write this book and others similar to it.

Our representatives have failed us and they unfortunately, are the most direct means of solving the problem. But, why will they? Good question! It always comes down to un-electing stubborn representatives who refuse to do the will of the people. Most people don't have the guts because something might happen to their nephews who hold government jobs. We get the government we deserve. If only others must sacrifice to clean up government, it will remain dirty.

Since the government is beginning to behave as an oligarchy and this was never the intention of the Founding Fathers as they drafted the Constitution, an injection of Direct Democracy might just be what the doctor ordered. It is fully in line with our U.S. Constitution, which vests ultimate sovereignty in the people, to create a mechanism that would permit the people back into our government process.

Our corrupt representatives have taken the people out of our democracy and some direct democracy principles can reinsert the people back into the scenario.

Through a constitutional amendment, for example, the people could gain the right to initiate national legislation (Initiative), create national referenda (Referendum), or demand the recall of officials (nowadays called scoundrels), who do not represent the people (Recall).

When the amendment passes, these activities could be sponsored by various public groups, or through the local and state governments. These three pillars of a direct democracy are presently reserved for the states whose constitutions specify these rights. It would be a relatively minor addition to our political system to engage the public in having a role in setting the political agenda. With how far our corrupt representatives have hijacked our national government, the time to act is now. We get the government we deserve.

Unfortunately, as noted above, not even all states have constitutions which permit the three prongs of a direct democracy. For example, my home state of Pennsylvania, has no statewide initiative or referendum rights, though Philadelphia and Allegheny (Pittsburgh) counties have it at the local level.

A group of Pennsylvanians called the "PA Taxpayers for Referendum Organization" are planning legislation to create a state constitutional convention to give PA these important rights. Many notable historical figures have suggested that our representative constitutional democracy could be improved with Initiative and Referendum. Their reasons seem to fit the national mood and the national need.

Theodore Roosevelt, for example, in his "Charter of Democracy" speech of 1912 said, "I believe in the initiative and referendum, which should be used not to destroy representative government, but to correct it whenever it becomes misrepresentative." Abraham Lincoln is well known for his words, "Government is of the people, for the people and by the people." Recall is a means of replacing government if the government does not act in a responsible way.

Back in 2005, the League of Women Voters of Pennsylvania took heed and offered that it "believes that citizens should have some means of taking direct action if their elected representatives fail to enact laws that voters support, or if they pass laws that are not wanted by the people." Does any of this hit home?

Whether at the state level or the federal level, any thought of the public as a whole being able to participate in the political agenda, with majority rule and one-vote-one-value, would send shivers down the spine of political operatives. The corporate owned corrupt media would go nuts. It would even appear to be a menace to all minority groups who today exercise disproportionate power through representatives.

But, fear not. As you know the Irish are a minority and I am Irish. The Catholics are a minority, and I am Catholic. As minority groups, this change would affect both of these groups, but maybe that is OK and for the greater good. I don't have a problem with the notion at all. It would actually be a way of controlling the idea often referred to as the tyranny of the minority in which the voice of a few have disproportionate power to their numbers over the many.

Watch Your Words; The Media 'll Get You

Elitists in the media and the bureaucracy who claim the right to know what's best for us every day pour forth a deluge of abuse and character assassination arguments to keep "We the People" in our place. In the 2008 presidential election, for example, the media anointed Senator McCain as the winner of the GOP nomination after Super Tuesday, though my state, Pennsylvania, and many other states had yet to express their opinions on the matter.

These volleys and even attacks don't come from nowhere. They come from the power-packed corporatocracy that owns the corrupt media. Watch what they say a little more carefully if you please, because they slander anybody who disagrees with them or who can alter their grip on power and propaganda. Though I believe that John McCain was a better choice than Barack Obama, I have learned enough about McCain since then that I feel his presidency would not have achieved greater results. John McCain is no Donald Trump.

In a 2019 book, such as this, we should not be talking about John Edwards or John McCain but we all learn from history. Some think that John Edwards' story and how he was summarily removed from the primary elections right from the beginning is actually a case study for the abuse of corporate power. When the powerful do not like somebody who is imperfect, they know how to slither in a less-capable person and they know how to make the terrible seem like Superman. You and I cannot pay for the ads needed to do that.

Today without ads the Democrats are ready to impeach one of their own 50-year public service champions. Joe Biden is getting the short-shrift all of a sudden from his Party because they no longer want him. Heck, he is a white male and "he is old."

Back when, Edwards, though selfishly motivated was a real champion against the established corporate power chieftains. He was a kick-butt trial lawyer who ate corporate chieftains for breakfast and salted away a huge nest egg of Kabul-licks for himself. He was defamed by the corporation-owned media simply because he was a "nasty" trial-lawyer. The real reason was so good at what he did as a lawyer, that he was a threat to their livelihood.

The irony is that the Democratic Party was and is still in bed with the trial lawyers. They wanted nothing to do with Edwards' promises to end the problems of "greedy corporations." Media surrogates instantly plopped the "trial-lawyer" label on Edwards and he was gone even before Super Tuesday.

Since the election of course, we all learned a few more leaked sordid details about John Edwards to make us feel good that corporate America destroyed him. but perhaps we were the people duped before Super Tuesday by the corrupt media? We get the government we deserve.

Corporations have begun a huge threat to our democracy and they need to be toned down a good measure so that real little guys do not feel their sting and so companies, such as General Electric do not have undue influence on our lives through their media holdings.

Way back in 2009, Forbes declared GE as the largest corporation in the world. There was a time that GE controlled NBC and MSNBC and CNBC. This level of control gave the corporate behemoth a little more influence on American life than is good for the people.

The Brave New World

Note: http://en.wikipedia.org/wiki/Brave_New_World,

Aldous Huxley wrote the Brave New World as a novel in 1932. The book is about the future and its setting is London, 2540 A.D. The novel anticipates that all of the reproductive advancements that today are just notions in a lab someplace, including biological engineering, and sleep-learning, will be commonplace in the future and will be used to change society.

The book talks about drug use as pacifiers to make the people feel better and loudspeakers used to get across the message. Later Huxley wrote two other books on the topic, one thirty years later in which he saw the future coming much sooner and the other, The Island, which took the sterile notions of Brave New World and made them more attractive and more positive. For example, loudspeakers are replaced by pleasing parrots trained to offer uplifting slogans.

Is our current day, " the Brave New World revisited," is a new deal in which the Government hands out pacifiers to keep the citizenry in a state of euphoria? What does such euphoria look like?

For the politician, it is a no-cost notion since they get elected by bribing you with your own money. Many citizens want there to be "no problems" so much so that they can't or won't listen to hear that there actually is a big problem that requires them to pay for its solution.

Yet, that is the system we have. Politicians who speak the truth are rejected because the voting public would rather be served denial and sugar and some pacifying stimuli. Ask Aldous Huxley, if you can find him.

Some people think Trump is the devil, but their facts are flimsy. I tend to think of Trump as an imperfect person who wishes he were a better man and who is hell-bent on becoming one. Sometimes we have to go back to know how close we were as a country to losing our identity.

Very early in the 2008 primaries we saw the media at work with sugar packets for those of us that don't mind being fat and Splenda for the slender among us. The media early on picked John McCain and Hillary Clinton as the only viable candidates. They just as quickly and amazingly switched to Barack Obama, though they owed Hillary and they knew it.

The media, and the Independents took the Republican primary from the Republicans without a whimper and they brought their man McCain in from sure doom to be the Republican Primary victor.

Somehow, they found a faux conservative in the lot and that's what the Republicans got by going along to get along.

The utterly corrupt corporate media, the low ratings media I might add, helped voters come to the media way of thinking with a constant barrage of propaganda for their guys and against all the others. The sinister part of the deal is that the propaganda sounded a lot like hard news. Intrinsically we all know that there is no free lunch but "don't ask me to pay!" We get the government we deserve.

Could we stomach the change we need?

Both parties each election spend more and more money to get elected then, while in office because they get rewarded for spending our money, they get reelected, which is reward enough. Even the Republican Party, though much more honest than the utterly corrupt Democrats, were big spenders during the Bush years. What was that all about?

Republicans and Democrats of course do not want to pay for spending with taxes, which affect their reelection opportunities, so they borrow and the poor, those on social security, the middle class and the rest of America pay the price by suffering with inflation.

The Democrats can always get a little more from the rich by implicitly invoking the subtle principles of class warfare. Both parties seem to have no problem borrowing from and bankrupting Social Security, which was supposed to have been in an Al Gore style, Lock Box.

Nobody talks about it because it serves no politician well, but the biggest tax is the inflation this spending behavior causes. There was no bigger spender in history than Barack Obama and his team of czars. Ironically, inflation is the worst and heaviest tax on the working poor. Each year, more Americans fall below the living wage because we pay for government's excessive spending with inflation and not taxes. Taxes were already high enough, but somebody had to pay for political pork (porkulus) and you know it would not be the politicians or the ruling class.

Each year the shrinking middle class fakes its standard of living by borrowing more, the only sensible thing when you have inflation. Greed of the ruling political class finished the Roman Empire and it is well lined up to finish the American economic empire. "Free healthcare" was almost been the final Obama-era nail in the US coffin.

Until the healthcare debate of 2009, I did not have overly high hopes that the electorate would opt to change anything as long as they too got something that benefitted them in the notion of "someone else will pay politics." The revolt of the summer of 2009 that has continued tells me that the people now seem more interested in the US as a surviving entity as any other issue I have ever seen.

The free lunch in 2018 is over folks. Until Barack Obama caricaturized government largesse with free-fall spending like never before, it seemed like many Americans, getting by barely, stubbornly were hanging on, sending back the political hacks for two more years or four more years or six more years, even when they chose not to represent us.

The sun seems to be shining on this folly now as more and more people are crying to throw the bums out. Trump was elected to eliminate a whole SWAMP of people. If he can, lots of normal people will cheer.

This downslide must end. It won't end, however, until we choose to end it at the ballot box and we forever hold the lesser "honorables" accountable or better yet, we just send them home to get real jobs like the rest of us.

The question always was, "do we have the stomach to do what is right?" Your friendly neighborhood politicians, all the way to the lords of the national ring are banking that you and I don't have the guts to do it. This time, I think they are wrong. We already brought Trump in at the top of the government.

The sleeping giants have been awakened. Americans are ready to fight another revolution to take America back. Perhaps we are not ready, but I think we are. Either way, we get the government we deserve.

Shall we cast off what is left of our independence and join the major political parties and ask for more government control and then we can loudly applaud our political leaders at important reelection functions? Maybe we can carry around their nominating petitions, and even hand out how-to-vote cards at elections.

Or, should we clamp down on this big problem with our democracy, speak up, demand action, and if we are not satisfied, now really, shouldn't we just throw the bums out?

Democracy is a relatively new phenomenon in its modern forms. It has developed over the last few centuries to a somewhat acceptable level in perhaps 40 of the world's 200-odd nation states. Judging from the U.S., it must further evolve. It cannot remain fixed in the face of accelerating change in all other aspects of society and the outright threat of takeover by corporate power and influence or as John Edwards correctly characterized it, "corporate greed."

The elements of direct democracy such as Initiative, Referendum, and Recall are anathema to politicians and governments at all levels. Yet, all three of these tenets could help enliven the political experience for the people and make government at all levels more accountable. In all western democracies, including the good ole U.S. of A., there are high levels of dissatisfaction.

Thus, there is more and more interest in politics by the yet-to-be-disillusioned young and things that can improve politics such as the Initiative amendment need to be brought forth and adopted. The mood of the country, voiced often by the young in the past presidential election brought forth the current administration and now the American people are getting changes many had never considered possible and every day it seems there is more.

The Bush years brought great division over the war in Iraq and a very unpopular president, from his own doing along with the help of the corrupt, left leaning media. So, now, we have trillions of dollars of debt, give-away programs for the rich (Wall street and the Bankers) that are better than PowerBall, and a never-ending big war in in the Middle East that until Mad Dog Mattis showed up did not seem like it would ever end.

We also have a CIA that was being emasculated and politicized by Obama, and we seem to have no fear at all of terrorism as the name during the former president's administration was even stricken from the federal dictionary. It seems that Michele and Barack had begun to live with Alice and the Tin Man to not notice that the America they shepherded was crumbling. On top of the new stuff, there is still the same old deep division in this country about open borders, the full response to terrorism, and the ongoing Iraq and Afghanistan wars. I fear these are just a few symptoms of a much deeper malaise. Thankfully for now, President Trump has these all on his agenda.

Familiarity Breeds Contempt

People everywhere seem to want to push the bounds of democracy further than their governments will allow. Back when, it was clear that both Prime Minister Blair in the UK and President Bush in the U.S. in their day, led incredibly unpopular governments. But they are of the past and thankfully new guys eventually took their places.

Gordon Brown got off to a great start as the #1 in the UK and our own Barack Obama was so popular he was almost declared a King and ruler for life in America until the 2016 election. Americans actually loved everything about the Obama family, from the kids to the new dog. Brown is not part of the dustbin of history.

Never have I seen such a high level of satisfaction for any President. Brits, sick of Tony Blaire and the Iraq War, were likewise quite pleased with Gordon Brown, though eventually he too had to go. And now we have Theresa May whose slipperiness may pull a no-Brexit out of a Brexit vote. Even Obama's time came due.

In addition to the big new rap of fiscal irresponsibility, the dissatisfaction with the U.S. government at all levels stems from many reasons such as a steady slide in social, economic and environmental conditions in the past 20 years; the increasingly overt nepotism, careerism, cronyism and outright corruption in our political system and in the government, itself.

Who do you trust? What once was a Johnny Carson game show tease, is now a question that beckons to be answered well but seemingly cannot be. In 2009, more and more blog contributions were asking, "Do you trust your government?" We keep asking it today.

On top of a major dislike for having unpopular notions rammed down the public's collective throat, much of this is fueled by public revulsion at brain-numbing political campaigns, the blatant disregard for the public in official decision-making, the dominance of big business, big unions, and big government, the flaunting of wealth by the ruling class, and increasingly fat salaries for politicians.

Meanwhile the general public (that's us) is chopped liver, theoretically living beyond its means, and we all have no recourse but to work harder for less money. With the economic collapse of late 2008, living beyond ones means has actually taken on new meaning and many individuals have been forced to follow this mantra.

Not to be outdone, the Federal government still finds no need at all to have a balanced checkbook, and those trying to balance theirs find it a bit disingenuous of our politicians to take pay raises while they are systematically draining the US treasury for their pet reelection projects. Is Nero fiddling again?

We the people have to tighten our belts to compete with those foreigners who would take our jobs while living either legally or illegally in the U.S., as well as those who would be pleased to do their jobs in China, India, or Russia or a host of developing nations. It's not pretty on the streets. " Let them eat cake" seemed to be the government response until the new Trump Administration. .

The public in ever increasing numbers, is also recognizing the structural defects of its political system. The centralization of power within the major parties so that there is no longer a two-party system nor room for independents is becoming quite obvious. Bush, Clinton, Bush, Clinton was almost not just a bad joke; it was almost a reality. Former president Barack Obama benefited on that one.

Add to all of this bad stuff the negativism and personal abuse inherent in adversary partisan politics, the domination of public decision-making by small elites, major party collusion depriving the public of choice, an institutionalized "broken promise syndrome," the failure of the government to be able to handle organized minority groups--legal and illegal--and undemocratic electoral systems and machines where only by chance, and sometimes in spite of devious manipulation, does the resulting government reflect the will of the people.

When representatives of the government from the Democrat Party call citizens at Town Hall meetings Astroturfers, and disingenuous, and at the same time they send their bought and paid for thugs and operatives (yes, the operatives of our legislators vs. the people) to combat and disrupt the "undue influence" of John Q Public on the fair and open legislative process, isn't this really an awful ugly pot calling the kettle names. Did anybody mention the words "healthcare," and "government control?"

In a democracy, it is axiomatic that the majority can only govern with the consent of the minority. Yet it helps to have a majority. Our last set of presidential elections show that there is a deep divide in this country. Yet until Trump, the good old boys in Congress (The SWAMP) sought bipartisan labels for their "solutions." It makes no sense since the biggest problem may just well be the political parties that breed our representatives.

The fact that the Democrats cannot accept defeat and have conjured up a number of faux methods to convince the people that their elected president is illegitimate is simply outrageous and un-American. Nobody but a Democrat likes a sore loser. Though the Mueller Report exonerated our President, the Democrats do not accept it and are having more fun trying to "get" Trump than they are doing their jobs in Congress.

Each new Congress seems to never be able to consider electoral matters except in terms of their partisan advantage. Underlying the alienation and powerlessness people feel is the lack of a true representative democracy, the accelerating rate of change since the 1980s, the information revolution, the forces of corporate globalization and the ongoing tyranny of the minorities. And they were the good ole days.

The best solution for the people is to stay awake and watch them like hawks. Throw them out when they get too big for their britches.

Chapter 8 Begging for Help at the Southern Border

Kirstjen Nielsen Wants Immediate Action

For the last six months I had been hearing that Department of Homeland Secretary Kirstjen Nielsen's job was in jeopardy. Other than CNN giving her a hard time just because she is part of the Trump Administration, the things I see indicate she is doing a great job, working hard, and doing the best she can. Of course, she is hamstrung just like the President is--because of a recalcitrant Congress. I am not sure what the President sees but she is surely in the news a lot in recent days as we get through the 2019 April Fool's Day period and we are on to Easter.

On April 2, for example, she convened an emergency conference call with members of President Donald Trump's Cabinet to discuss migration at the southern border. This is a big emergency for the country that Democrats are enjoying because they want more and more illegal aliens in the country. They might not want to ride in the caravans but Dems they want the caravans to make it to New York unimpeded by US laws.

"We are going to treat it as if we have been hit by a Cat 5 hurricane," Nielsen said on the call. There are 900,000 people this year coming without any legal right to stay."

She told Cabinet members that Homeland Security is establishing an "emergency operations cell" as is done during a hurricane with daily video teleconferences and operational updates, the source said.

It is such an emergency for the safety of the country that Nielsen has clearly been stepping up the administration's response to the surge in migrants crossing the southern US border. They are all illegal.

Just the day before, she had left bilateral security meetings with European officials early and bowed out of the G7 Interior Ministers' Meeting in Paris. She headed right back to Washington to continue managing the situation at the southern border.

Additionally, she directed CBP (Customs & Border Protection) to speed up its planned surge of at least 750 officers to assist Border Patrol along areas of the southern border. Nielsen also ordered that CBP immediately expand Homeland Security's policy of returning asylum-seekers to Mexico for the duration of their immigration proceedings.

All of this action is concurrent with President Donald Trump's consideration to shut down the southern border or levying a 35% tariff on Mexican car imports or both. The threat is on the table that he will do so if Mexico does not begin / continue apprehending more undocumented migrants from coming into the US. As discussed in prior days, Trump already said the US is cutting off aid to the Central American countries of El Salvador, Guatemala and Honduras, otherwise known as the Northern Triangle.

On top of all that, Secretary Nielson has asked for immediate action from Congress to address the dire situation at the border. This includes new authority to immediately deport unaccompanied minors back to their home countries. Her department is on the firing line to get a lot done in the US battle for the border. "Now we face a system-wide meltdown," Nielsen wrote in a letter recently obtained.

Responding to President Trump's recent threats to completely close the southern border, Nielsen will advise Trump on how to implement a full shutdown.

"I will make a recommendation accordingly to the President," she said. Nielsen acknowledged that children who cross the border and end up in U.S. custody "are being put at risk" as shelters hit max capacity.

Under current department policy, unaccompanied minors can be sent back if they're from originally from Mexico. The Secretary's request for new Homeland Security authority would allow unaccompanied children from other countries to be removed just as easily.

"The idea here is asking Congress to treat all children the same," Nielsen said Friday. I do not expect Congress to help Nielson as anything that helps the border situation hurts the goals of the Democrats who now control the House. They want more and more voters and anything that hurts Trump they feel helps Democrats even as it hurts the country.

Border Patrol has struggled to fully enforce security measures while transporting and caring for the record high numbers of migrants crossing without authorization

The Letter to Congress as written by the Secretary

This letter was sent Thursday March 28 2019 to each member of our Congress by the Secretary of Homeland Security, Kirstjen M. Nielsen. It has not received much publicity because the press is corrupt and they are rooting against Trump as well as rooting for the members of the illegal caravan / onslaught of immigrants encroaching our borders. I have read pleas for help before and this letter is very complete and it surely paints a dire picture. One must believe the corrupt Press wants the US to fail.

How can Congress think they know more than the Director of Homeland Security? Yet, they act that way. Why will Congress not act to help both America and the immigrants who suffer on their way to a life with a low wage or welfare in the US? They must know that their permissive actions act as a magnet for people across the world who come and then wonder where the milk and honey they were promised actually may be.

I would tell the "migrants" who become illegal aliens to go into the gated communities where the Congress Members live and ask them for that milk and honey and I hope they get some.

Please send a note to your Congress Members when you have a chance and ask what they plan to do! Hopefully, they will have read it by then. Send this letter from Ms. Nielson with it.

Secretary

U.S. Department of Homeland Security
Washington, DC 20528

Homeland Security

March 28, 2019

United States Senate
Washington DC 20515

U.S House of Representatives
Washington DC 20515

Dear Members of Congress:

I am writing to you with an urgent request. For many months now, the Department of Homeland Security (DHS) has been tracking a surge in migrant arrivals at the U.S. southern border. It is the responsibility of DHS to secure our borders, enforce our immigration laws, and provide appropriate humanitarian protections to those who need it. Indeed, Congress has explicitly directed DHS to take operational control of the southern border. But today I report to you that we are increasingly unable to uphold that responsibility given the emergency situation. We are grappling with a humanitarian and security catastrophe that is worsening by the day, and the Department has run out of capacity, despite extraordinary intra-Departmental and interagency efforts. I am especially concerned about the level of families and unaccompanied children arriving at our borders and in federal custody. Accordingly, DHS requests immediate Congressional assistance to stabilize the situation.

The border numbers paint a picture of a dire situation. Late last year, DHS was apprehending 50,000 - 60,000 migrants a month. Last month, we apprehended or encountered more than 75,000, the highest in over a decade. And this month, we are on track to interdict nearly 100,000 migrants. What we are seeing is nearly unprecedented in the modern era. Unlike previous flows, these migrants are not arriving in high numbers, one-at-a-time. They are arriving in large groups. In a normal year, DHS would encounter one or two groups of over 100 migrants. Already in this fiscal year, we have encountered nearly 100 large groups comprised of 100+ migrants, nearly half of which have arrived in remote locations. Our men and women on the frontlines are simply not resourced to handle these levels, and I report to you today that we are struggling to transport and process-let alone adequately care for this many individuals coming into our custody, especially those in hard-to-reach areas.

The volume of "vulnerable populations" is unsustainable. Our system has been able to cope with high numbers in the past, but the composition of today's flows makes them virtually unmanageable. Historically, the vast majority of aliens we encountered were single-adult males from Mexico who could be quickly removed after a short period of detention if they had no legal right to stay. Today, the majority are families and unaccompanied children, who pose a unique challenge to the system because most cannot be easily cared for, efficiently processed, or expeditiously removed, due to resource constraints and outdated laws. The result is a dangerous and growing backlog of individuals in custody that has forced us to begin releasing large numbers of aliens, most of whom will never appear for their immigration court hearings, further exacerbating "pull" factors into the United States. Unfortunately, Alternatives to Detention, such as ankle-bracelet monitoring, have proven expensive in the long run and ineffective at ensuring removals ordered by an immigration judge.

Now we face a system-wide meltdown. DHS facilities are overflowing, agents and officers are stretched too thin, and the magnitude of arriving and detained aliens has increased the risk of life-threatening incidents. At the present time, Customs and Border Protection (CBP) has more than 1,200 unaccompanied alien children (UACs) in custody, hundreds of which have been with CBP for days, an unacceptable length of stay in facilities not designed to hold children for extended periods. By law, most of these children must be transferred to the Department of Health and Human Services (HHS) for care in residential shelters. While HHS is taking steps to rapidly add thousands of shelter beds, the system is hitting peak capacity. In addition to UACs, CBP has at least 6,600 families in custody, bringing the total number of children sitting in CBP facilities to approximately 4,700. We are doing everything possible to address these numbers and reduce backlogs, but they are a symptom of a broken system.

My greatest concern is for the children, who arc put at high risk by this emergency and who are arriving sicker than ever before after traveling on the treacherous trek. Our agents and officers are performing more than 60 hospital visits a day—many to ensure young people get immediate treatment and we now are regularly seeing individuals arrive with life-threatening conditions. Moreover, as agents get pulled off the line to escort migrants to receive medical assistance, we are left with even less capacity. To handle new arrivals. The humanitarian situation cannot be ignored. Reports of violence and sexual assault along the route are now pervasive, meaning that many arriving migrants require especially focused care. In some cases, girls as young as 10 years old in DHS custody require pregnancy tests so we can be sure they get essential medical support. And, with increased flows, smugglers and traffickers are forcing more people into inhumane conditions as long the journey and putting lives in danger. They are preying on innocent people for profit and exploiting this crisis to line their pockets by breaking our laws.

Our most urgent need is to increase throughput to avoid threats to life and property. At present, DHS border and immigration facilities are at (or over) capacity with serious over-crowding. We need additional temporary facilities as soon as possible in order to process arriving aliens, especially those entering illegally between ports of entry.

[In general, a port of entry (POE) is a place where one may lawfully enter a country. ... International airports are usually ports of entry, as are road and rail crossings on a land border. Seaports can be used as ports of entry only if a dedicated customs presence is posted there.]

Immigration and Customs Enforcement (ICE) has been urgently working to acquire additional bed space and to speed up transfers of individuals into their custody, but DHS has nonetheless been forced to temporarily release adults and families directly from Border Patrol custody. This prevents us from detaining them to assure that they are afforded the most expeditious process under immigration law and, where appropriate, removed. Without additional assistance, we will be forced to increase the releases of the single-adult population from ICE the only population for which we can currently effectively enforce US immigration laws. As such, we are witnessing real-time dissolution of the immigration system.

Moreover, HHS will likely need many more beds as the influx of children grows. In HHS custody, children receive accommodations appropriate for young people while they await placement with adult sponsors in the United States. However, because of the surge in arrivals, CBP has high numbers of children that have not been transferred. As noted earlier, HHS is taking steps to rapidly add thousands of shelter beds. But in the short term, HHS is still approaching its maximum capacity and will very likely require thousands of additional beds in the coming weeks and months. I must emphasize how important it is to quickly transfer children out of border locations, which are not designed for long-term stay and are especially inadequate for the care of young people. A potential overflow of children in DHS custody represents our most acute humanitarian risk.

But bed space is not the only issue. To cope with the overall volume of arriving migrants, a resource surge is needed throughout the system to ensure efficient throughput and proper care. This includes medical teams, vehicles and transportation workers, legal services, and more. We need temporary processing facilities with full humanitarian and staffing support. And we now project that we will need at least hundreds of additional personnel to support CBP and ICE in providing humanitarian and operational assistance, including conducting welfare checks, preparing meals, and accounting for personal property.

In light of the above, DHS requests immediate assistance from Congress, including emergency resources and specific authorities to cope with the escalating situation.

At this time, DHS is assessing the resources needed to make up for shortfalls and sustain critical operations. While recent appropriations provided DHS with additional humanitarian and operational funds, the Department is projecting we will exceed these resources and be unable to uphold basic mission requirements because of the severity of the flow. I will be working with the Office of Management and Budget to provide you additional details in the near future, but the situation is so dire we want to make notification to you now that we will require additional resources to reduce system backlogs to ensure immediate safety and care of individuals in our custody.

DHS also seeks authorities to address the underlying causes of this emergency and to restore order, while ensuring we can provide humanitarian assistance to those who need it. Most immediately, we need the authority to treat all arriving migrant children equally. Currently, we can reunite many unaccompanied children from Mexico with their families and return them home, when appropriate, but we are legally unable to do so for children from noncontiguous countries. The result is that hundreds of Central American children come into our custody each day, await transfer to HHS care, and, ultimately, are placed with a sponsor in the United States. This serves as another dangerous "pull" factor. DHS seeks authority to return UACs to their families and home countries in a safe and orderly manner if they have no legal right to stay. In the coming days, I will transmit proposed legislative language to Congress to fix this, along with measures to allow DHS to keep alien families in custody together through the immigration process and to allow asylum-seekers to apply for U.S. protection from within Central America, rather than take the dangerous journey north. These legislative solutions will help address the root causes of the emergency.

In the meantime, I am doing everything within my authority to

prevent the situation from getting worse. This week I met with senior Mexican officials to discuss what can be done on their side of the border to help stem the historic flows. I also signed a first-ever regional compact with the countries of the Northern Triangle-El Salvador, Guatemala, and Honduras to address irregular migration, counter human smuggling and trafficking, and crack down on transnational criminal organizations that are also fueling the crisis. Operationally, we are redirecting resources and personnel from across the Department toward border security and migration management, we are putting out a call for volunteers from non-border missions, and we continue to receive support from interagency partners. We also plan to redirect field office personnel staffing ports of entry to help address the humanitarian situation. But once again, this will not be enough.

We need Congress to act immediately to address the growing emergency. Let me be clear: the journey of any migrant--especially at the hands of a smuggler or traffickeris not a safe one. And the migrant surge has made matters worse, not only for U.S. border security but for the safety of migrants themselves. We must be able to come together on a bipartisan basis to take action. We have common cause. We all want to enforce the laws of the United States, ensure a safe and orderly migrant flow, protect our communities, reduce the flow of drugs, facilitate legal trade and travel, secure our borders, and support vulnerable populations. This is one of the most serious crises the Department of Homeland Security has ever faced, and we need your help.

Copies of this letter have been sent to the Speaker of the House; the Majority and Minority Leaders in the Senate and House; and the Chairmen and Ranking Members of the Senate Appropriations Committee, Senate Judiciary Committee, Senate Homeland Security and Governmental Affairs Committee, House Appropriations Committee, House Judiciary Committee, and House Homeland Security Committee.

Respectfully,

Kirstjen M. Nielsen
Secretary

Secretary Kirstjen Nielsen Statement on Border Emergency

This memo was written the following day, March 29, 2019:

Release Date:

March 29, 2019

WASHINGTON, D.C. - Secretary of Homeland Security Kirstjen M. Nielsen made the following statement today on the situation at the U.S. southern border and how the Department of Homeland Security (DHS) is responding:

"Today I report to the American people that we face a cascading crisis at our southern border. The system is in freefall. DHS is doing everything possible to respond to a growing humanitarian catastrophe while also securing our borders, but we have reached peak capacity and are now forced to pull from other missions to respond to the emergency."

"Let me be clear: the volume of 'vulnerable populations' arriving is without precedent. This makes it far more difficult to care for them and to prioritize individuals legitimately fleeing persecution. In the past, the majority of migration flows were single adults who could move through our immigration system quickly and be returned to their home countries if they had no legal right to stay. Now we are seeing a flood of families and unaccompanied children, who—because of outdated laws and misguided court decisions—cannot receive efficient adjudication and, in most cases, will never be removed from the United States even if they are here unlawfully. The result is a massive 'pull factor' to our country."

"My gravest concern is for children. They are arriving sicker than ever before and are exploited along the treacherous trek. Smugglers and traffickers know that our laws make it easier to enter and stay if you show up as a family. So they are using children as a 'free ticket' into America, and have in some cases even used kids multiple times—recycling them—to help more aliens get into the United States. Our border stations were not designed to hold young people for extended periods, yet this influx has forced thousands of them into facilities that are getting crowded and overwhelmed. This goes well beyond politics. We must come together to find a way to tackle the crisis and reduce the flows so children are not put at risk. Any system that encourages a parent to send their child alone on this terrible journey—where they are exploited, pawned, and recycled—is completely broken."

"Moreover, our agents and officers at the border cannot fulfill their critical national security responsibilities while also attending to the influx of vulnerable populations. That is why, effective immediately, I am redirecting additional personnel and resources from across the Department to assist with the response, I have put out a call Department-wide for volunteers to provide support to our frontline agencies, and I am appealing to interagency partners for further assistance. But it will not be enough, so this week I notified Congress that DHS will need emergency legislative action to restore order, achieve operational control of our border, and ensure we can fulfill our humanitarian responsibilities effectively."

"Make no mistake: Americans may feel effects from this emergency. As personnel are reallocated to join the crisis-response effort, there may be commercial delays, higher vehicle wait times at the border, and longer pedestrian lines. Despite these impacts, we cannot shirk our responsibility to the American people to do everything possible to secure our country while also upholding our humanitarian values." Secretary Nielsen sent a letter yesterday to Congress highlighting the severity of the crisis, especially the danger posed to children by the journey to U.S. borders and the realities of a system reaching peak capacity. This week, after many months of diplomatic negotiations, Secretary Nielsen signed a historic regional compact

<u>this week</u> with representatives of the Northern Triangle—El Salvador, Guatemala, and Honduras—to confront the crisis at the source. The countries agreed to work with the United States to combat human smuggling and trafficking, crack down on transnational criminals fueling the crisis, and strengthen border security to prevent irregular migration. The Secretary also <u>met with senior officials from the Government of Mexico</u> to discuss ways to quickly address the crisis and stem historic migration flows through Mexican territory, while ensuring all individuals legitimately fleeing persecution receive appropriate humanitarian protection.

Secretary Nielsen Orders CBP to Surge More Personnel to Southern Border, Increase Number of Aliens Returned to Mexico

Here is a memo from April 1st on more personnel for taking care of border matters.

Release Date:

April 1, 2019

Today, Homeland Security Secretary Kirstjen M. Nielsen issued a memorandum to U.S. Customs and Border Protection (CBP) Commissioner Kevin McAleenan outlining new steps the agency must take to combat the growing security and humanitarian crisis at the southern border.

"The crisis at our border is worsening, and DHS will do everything in its power to end it," said Secretary Nielsen. "We will not stand idly by while Congress fails to act yet again, so all options are on the table. We will immediately redeploy hundreds of CBP personnel to the border to respond to this emergency. We will urgently pursue additional reinforcements from within DHS and the interagency. And we will require those seeking to enter the United States to wait in Mexico until an immigration court as reviewed their claims."

The Secretary ordered Commissioner McAleenan to undertake emergency surge operations and immediately increase its temporary reassignment of personnel and resources from across the agency to address the influx of migrants. According to the directive, the CBP Office of Field Operations shall accelerate its planned reallocation of up to 750 officers to Border Patrol Sectors that are affected by the emergency. Moreover, CBP is directed to explore raising that target, is authorized to exceed it, and shall notify the Secretary if reassignments are planned to exceed 2,000 personnel.

Secretary Nielsen further directed CBP to immediately expand the Migrant Protection Protocols (MPP), a DHS initiative to return aliens to Mexico to wait during the pendency of their U.S. immigration proceedings. The Secretary directed CBP to return hundreds of additional migrants per day above current rates to Mexico, consistent with U.S. law and humanitarian obligations. This increase in returns shall include individuals apprehended or encountered at or between POEs. Moreover, the agency is directed to plan for an expansion of MPP beyond the locations in which it currently operates in California and Texas.

Last Published Date: April 2, 2019

On April 7, 2019, the situation at the border changed in that Secretary Neilson resigned as DHS Director. President Trump announced Sunday afternoon that Homeland Security Secretary Kirstjen Nielsen "will be leaving her position" 16 months in the job. Trump also announced that U.S. Customs and Border Protection (CBP) Commissioner Kevin McAleenan will replace Nielsen as acting secretary, tweeting: "I have confidence that Kevin will do a great job!"

The Flores Settlement is the :law" that regulates the detention, release, and treatment of children in the custody of federal immigration authorities. Nielsen was not responsible for Flores.

We can thank Democrats continual lying and blaming and complaining for Nielsen's resignation. With insistence that the Flores agreement, be enforced to the letter and then creating negative press when it was enforced, Democrat lies helped bring a fine Trump official under fire and ultimately forced her resignation. Lies, Lies, Democrat lies. Nielsen never put children in cages. Lies Lies Lies, Democrat lies hurt people and they hurt the country.

Chapter 9 Before California Mexicans, came the Chinese

Chinese workers on the Transcontinental Railroad circa 1850

Americans often benefit from exploitation

California always has had a large population of illegal migrant workers. They have great soil, a great climate, and they produce crops for all of America. Californians welcomed help from friends in Mexico for years to help them with their harvests. Whether this was something that helped everyday Californians at the time; quite frankly, I admit that I do not know. But it seems that the relationship was symbiotic.

Some of you, who have been to Nevada County and Oroville California may be familiar with the Chinese Temple and other remnants of the bygone age of the Chinese Miners. The Temple was reopened in 1949 as a California State Park, more or less as a monument to days long past as the country was being built.

This particular site and others like it had been abandoned in the 1880's when the Chinese miners or railroad workers who lived there returned to China about the time that the Transcontinental Railroad was completed. There is a parallel with today's southern invasion of the US.

The Chinese came to America in the 1800s because of a poor situation in their home country. Like the Irish after the great famine, many Mexicans and those from Central and South America looking for relief found refuge in America. The Chinese and others sent money home regularly and, unlike the Irish, they did not assimilate into the American culture of the day.

Their culture may have been even more isolated than that of today's illegal immigrant. The Chinese reaction to America was a big first dose of the value of borders for Americans watching the impact on language and culture. American officials did not get it then and still do not get it.

Unlike today's illegal immigrants from the south, when their work was done, the Chinese went home. They did not want to change US culture into a Chinese culture. For example, they had no desire for everyone to speak and act Chinese. There was no movement for example to press 1 for English, 2 for Mandarine, or 3 for Cantonese, etc.

In their heyday, the Chinese had quite a thing going in California. Like the Mexicans, they provided a reliable source of inexpensive labor to US industry and they offered a wide range of services. The Chinese were industrious and smart and they really knew how to make a buck. For example, they offered laundries, garden fresh vegetables, firewood and of course domestic services. They worked very hard for all they achieved. They were never on the taxpayer dole. Today's illegal residents could learn a lesson from the Chinese of yore.

Because their primary work was as miners and railroad builders, they also bought tools, supplies and mining equipment from American manufacturers. They also paid taxes. Nobody had to carry them. They made it on their own. Americans like those who make it on their own and typically do not like those who dip into their wallets and purses for support. c

Nevada County, California reports they collected $103,250.00 in Foreign Miners Tax almost exclusively from the Chinese between 1850 and 1870. Think about its worth in today's inflated dollars. Unlike today's illegal aliens, and this is a lesson for those who stay illegally in America, they did not rely on a government infrastructure (schools, hospitals, etc.). And, so it did not cost Americans every day for the Chinese to live and work in the US.

When the Transcontinental Railroad was mostly completed in 1869, thousands of Chinese became unemployed along with a lot of Americans. California, the end of the railroad line, went into an economic depression, and much like today, many blamed foreign nationals—the Chinese.

It was not their fault but the jobs were gone and American citizens believed they should hold all of the jobs that existed before any foreigner was hired or was permitted to continue to work. Unlike today, the US government took the side of the Americans.

I suspect the same thing would happen in China if there were no longer a need for foreign workers. There was little sympathy for the Chinese or any other foreign laborer when Americans had a pressing need to feed their families. For its own reasons, our Congress thinks Americans of today need no such protection?

Government did not act immediately. However, when things had not improved by 1882, the Congress passed the Chinese Exclusion Act. This legislation suspended the immigration of "laborers" and prohibited naturalization of the Chinese who sought American citizenship as it was deemed, they would make employment even more difficult for Americans in the hard times of the day. There is no question that today's Congress would not support such legislation to help American workers. Today's Congress represents itself and not the people. Ask Nancy Pelosi.

American legislators at the time worked for the good of America, not other countries that tried to gain employment for their citizens. For Americans today, having a government that works for American citizens is a foreign notion. Our lawmakers do not work for

Americans. One day we will all wake up and fire our legislators. I hope it is not too late.

There was no notion at the time of anchor babies (automatic citizenship for babies born in America) since Chinese women rarely came to America while their husbands provided 100% labor for industry. The men worked hard and had simple pleasures in life, including brothels. The Chinese mostly stayed away from any potential conflict with Americans other than wanting their jobs when there were no jobs at all.

As noted, unlike today, the US government was pro-American at the time, and Americans came first. When there were not enough jobs for both Chinese and Americans, it was the Chinese that had to go. There was no gang of eight tyrants serving as American legislators, who emerged ready to make Americans subservient to the Chinese.

The government, rightly or wrongly protected Americans in those days above foreigners. I say it was right. Instead of trying to figure out how to make it tougher for Americans who want to work, as our legislators, such as the gang of eight tyrants plotted just a few years ago, they should try to figure out how to best help America and Americans.

The US government made it so hard for Chinese to be employed when Americans were available to take the jobs that many Chinese men chose to return to China. There is another parallel of the Chinese with the southern migration to the US. After the Chinese Exclusion Act, Chinese who migrated to the US, despite the ban were looked upon similarly as illegal aliens today and were subject to deportation, and many were deported.

Should the government of the US today be protecting Americans in a similar way? Of course, only Americans are American!

The US government at that time was representing Americans and not Chinese. Today, for its own reasons, our government represents non-Americans to the detriment of American Citizens.

Historians are well aware that on Dec. 13, 1943, during WWII, President Franklin D. Roosevelt repealed the Chinese Exclusion Act because China had become such an important ally of the United States against Japan. Clearly the act was detrimental to Chinese immigrants. Yet, the small numbers that were in the country at that time could have and probably should have been made citizens. It was not the same situation as today.

Today, with 50 to 60 million or more illegal resident immigrants, even Franklin Roosevelt would see that this number could not be assimilated, even if all the king's horses and all the king's men were employed to make it happen.

The Chinese had notable successes in America, far greater than any religion, or ethnicity. They had built the Transcontinental Railroad for the good of America. Despite that, they were encouraged to go back to China. Americans were out of work and so it was understandable that sentiments were for the home country as it should be.

Before Trump, during the Obama years, there were millions of Americans out of work and many more choosing not to try again after years of knocking on Human Resource doors. The fact is today there are still as many as 60,000,000 illegal aliens in the country, if not more. The fact is that our government has decided that Americans are not as important as we once were. Things have clearly changed from the days when our government protected us from foreign invaders.

The irony is that as American Citizens, if we wish to use it, we have the ultimate power to send all of the bad legislators that have created our misfortunes back to their home states. Perhaps it is a bit overdue but it sure is time we did something.

Chapter 10 Every Illegal Alien Is a Criminal

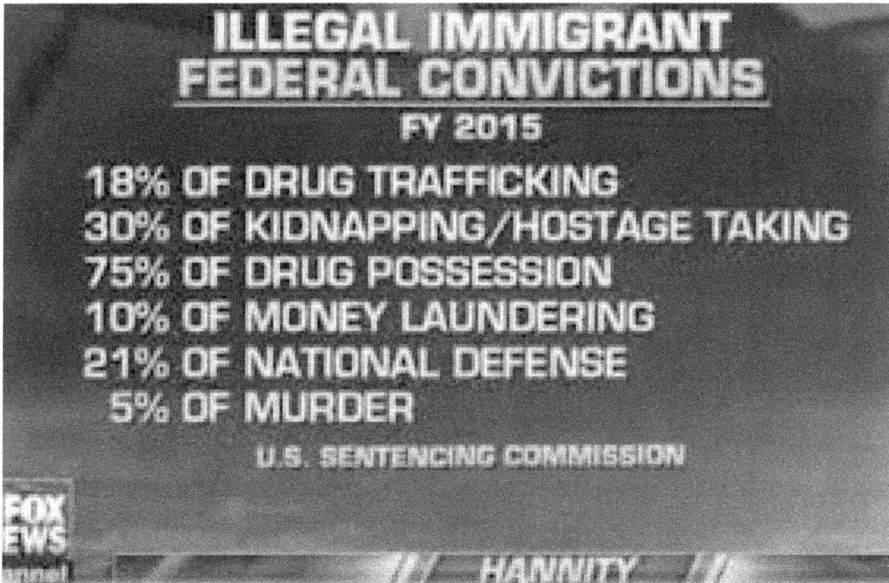

ILLEGAL IMMIGRANT FEDERAL CONVICTIONS
FY 2015
18% OF DRUG TRAFFICKING
30% OF KIDNAPPING/HOSTAGE TAKING
75% OF DRUG POSSESSION
10% OF MONEY LAUNDERING
21% OF NATIONAL DEFENSE
5% OF MURDER
U.S. SENTENCING COMMISSION

How many crimes does it take to make a criminal?

Just one folks! Just one! Every illegal alien is a criminal. They commit a crime to enter the country. A person who commits a crime obviously is willing to break the law. Does a person willing to commit one crime stop at one when there is no punishment? Do they know where to draw the lines when their very existence in the US is a crime? Do they feel they have a right to make their own laws?

Once in the US, an illegal foreign national may end up in, say, Pennsylvania, where I live. Pennsylvania is hard to get around unless you have a car. At least today, illegal immigrants are not permitted to have Pennsylvania drivers' licenses? Do they drive anyway? They sure do.

They pretty much have to drive to function in the stick-lands of Pennsylvania. We already know they are able and willing to break laws so why not break another by driving. Once driving without a license for a length of time, do you think they choose to buy insurance on their illegally registered vehicle? Insurance is required to drive in Pennsylvania, but who is counting the number of crimes needed to survive? Pity the PA driver that gets in an accident with one of these interlopers who choose to make their own laws.

Many, who advocate giving America away to foreigners claim, with no facts provided, that illegal foreign nationals commit fewer rimes than Americans. Of course, this is not true. Yet, it is difficult to find official statistics on people who are not officially in the country. As a sanctuary state, California has a very high population of illegal foreign nationals from China and south of the border.

What is a sanctuary city or state?

We hear the term sanctuary city often in discussion about illegal immigration. *Sanctuary city* is a term used across the world (French: ville sanctuaire; Spanish: ciudad santuario). It refers to municipal jurisdictions, typically in North America and Western Europe, that limit their cooperation with the national government's effort to enforce immigration law. As a sanctuary state, California's legislation prohibits law enforcement agents from asking about a person's immigration status or participating in any program that uses them as immigration agents. To many it is like the old outlaw towns of the old west where lawmen were not permitted and outlaws frolicked while spending their ill-gotten treasures.

Because they have had the problem for longer than most states, California's crime statistics are much more available than in other areas of the country. Some of the numbers that have been publicized in the last ten years make an ordinary person shudder. They include the following:

- In Los Angeles, ninety-five percent of about 1500 outstanding warrants for homicides are for illegal foreign nationals.
- Upwards of 67% of about 20,000 outstanding fugitive felony warrants are for illegal aliens.
- Illegal aliens marked for deportation fall through the cracks. Over 400,000 illegal alien criminals with deportation orders

have disappeared into thin air. One fourth or more of these are hard core criminals.
- Approximately 100,000 illegal foreign nationals, who have already gone to trial and have already been convicted are still walking the streets. Statistics for such repeat offenders are an average of 13 serious crimes per perpetrator.
- The bottom line is that illegal aliens are involved in criminal activities at a rate 2 to 5 times their representative proportion of the US population.
- As a telling statistic, way back in 1980, six years before the big Reagan amnesty, federal and state facilities held fewer than 9,000 criminal aliens. Yet, at the end of 2003, this number had ballooned to about 270,000 illegal aliens. These were incarcerated in U.S. correctional facilities at a cost of about $6.8 billion per year, and the numbers and the toll keep increasing.

There are also costs that society bears for protected foreign "outlaws." For example, the below statistics are from about six years ago. We can expect the numbers to be higher today:

- About 5 million pounds of cocaine with a street value of at least $80 billion is smuggled across the southern border every year.
- 56% of illegal aliens charged with a reentry offense had previously been convicted on at least 5 prior occasions.
- Illegal foreign nationals charged with unlawful reentry had the most extensive criminal histories. 90% had been previously arrested. Of those with a prior arrest, 50% had been arrested for violent or drug-related felonies.
- Illegal aliens commit between 700,000 to 1,289,000 or more crimes per year.
- Illegal aliens commit at least 2,158 murders each year – a number that represents three times greater participation than their proportion of the population.
- Illegal alien sexual predators commit an estimated 130,909 sexual crimes each year.
- There may be as many as 240,000 illegal alien sex offenders circulating throughout America. Based on studies,

they will commit an average of 8 sex crimes per perpetrator before being caught.

- Nearly 63% of illegal alien sex offenders had been deported on another offense prior to committing the sex crime.
- Only 2% of the illegal alien sex offenders in one study had no history of criminal behavior, beyond crossing the border illegally.
- In Operation Predator, ICE arrested and deported 6,085 illegal alien pedophiles. Some studies suggest each pedophile molests average of 148 children. If so, that could be as many as 900,580 victims.
- Nobody knows how big the Sex Slave problem is but it is enormous.
- The very brutal MS-13 gang has over 15,000 members and associates in at least 115 different cliques in 33 states.
- The overall financial impact of illegal alien crimes is estimated at between $15 and $100 billion or more per year. Factor in the crime as a result of the cocaine and other drugs being smuggled in and the number may reach $200 billion per year.

So, to those who once believed or were told that Americans commit more crimes than illegal foreign nationals; do you still feel this way? Do you still think illegal immigration is a "victimless crime" and we don't need to control our borders? Remember, about 60% of the crimes being committed by illegal aliens are interlopers who have been previously deported.

The Obama administration did not care what the statistics were or so it seemed. It decided early on in its tenure that Americans did not matter as much as foreign nationals. The objective was to bolster the Democrat voting bloc.

Thus, the past administration seemed to believe that the people did not need the protection of the government to secure the borders. Moreover, if a state, such as Arizona, chose to protect itself, the Obama Administration overtly took action against them and would sue them since apparently the Democrats believe that foreigners have more rights than American citizens.

Most Americans at the time trusted the government and wimpy RINOs were afraid to take a stance. Therefore, Obama got his work done on behalf of illegal aliens, mostly unimpeded

In late 2012, the Obama team quietly put out a memo to ICE personnel who are charged with assuring our border security. They told them not to try so hard anymore because illegal foreign nationals are really good fellows and do not need the big stick of ICE coming down on them too heavily.

Officially, the memo stated that the U.S. Immigration and Customs Enforcement (ICE) agency will no longer detain or seek to deport illegal aliens charged with misdemeanor crimes.

Among the conditions under which ICE agents became permitted to issue a detainer, were if "the individual had three or more prior misdemeanor convictions." Please note the word convictions. Supposedly, there were a few exceptions to the new policy, including those charged with, or convicted of a DUI and sexual abuse. But, the fact that Big Sis (Janet Napolitano, DHS Chief) had full discretion on who leaves and who stays and she was quite lenient, was an affront to all Americans.

The memo was signed by John Morton, the director of U.S. Immigration and Customs Enforcement and released on a Friday evening so it would not clutter the weekly news. The Obama administration tried most of the time to cover up its tracks and leave nothing to chance from a PR perspective. It had become well known for its so-called 'Friday night document dumps.' This was a long-practiced Obama trick to not draw attention to the unpopular or damning information contained in the necessary press release.

The Obama spokesman Morton said in this latest release that the memo restricts action "against individuals arrested for minor misdemeanor offenses." Wow, that is insult upon injury. Obama is not a dictator and had no right to suspend any law passed by Congress or any article or right in the Constitution. It seems like he and his administration missed that particular memo from the founders.

Murder is a way of life for some

How many people are murdered by illegal aliens per day? Ask Kate Steinle in heaven because she has the exact count. Ask her parents, who weep to this day. José Inez García Zárate only knows that he snuffed out Kate's life and hopefully cannot report on other murders. This illegal alien claimed a gun had fired accidentally while he was picking it up; he also claimed he had found the gun moments before. Folks, how many times has a situation like this happened to you?

Would you be surprised if the statistics clearly indicate that at least twelve Americans are murdered every day by illegal aliens? Representative Steve King, R-Iowa is on top of the statistics which were released from his office. This translates to 4,380 Americans murdered annually by illegal aliens. Is that an emergency? That's 52, 560 since Sept. 11, 2001. These murderers are hardly innocent people who simply need a nice place to live.

There are also a number of illegal foreign national murdering criminals who really did not intend to commit murder; but did so anyway. As reported above, Congressman King notes that 12 Americans are murdered daily by illegal aliens. Another 13 daily are killed by drunk illegal alien drivers. So, we have another annual death total of 4,745 on top of the 4,380.. That's 56,940 additional Americans in graves because of drunk illegal aliens since Sept. 11, 2001.

In total, without adding those that are unreported, there have been well over 100,000 killed at a rate of over 9,000 per year, and it is not expected to end any time soon, regardless of what happens in the future if the gang of eight tyrants' bill is ever resurrected. Nonetheless, it is a big problem that should be considered before anybody gets a path to citizenship.

Examples of Serious Crimes of Illegal Aliens

Fairus.org—aka the Federation for American Immigration reform studies all sides of the immigration debate and are a very good source for immigration statistics. They compiled a list of serious crimes committed by illegal aliens to refute the notion that these interlopers do no harm on their journey as residents of America. I have included their data for 2013 below in reverse chronological order to close out this chapter.

FAIR gets their information from various news sources. In the list of crimes shown below, the aliens involved in these reports were all identified as being in the country illegally. Many of them had come into the hands of law enforcement agencies prior to the crime that is described below, but the alien was not deported or in some cases was deported but reentered the country.

These cases are listed as a demonstration that better prevention of illegal immigration is a public safety issue even though these cases are not representative of the illegal alien population in general. These cases refer to crimes other than terrorism. Remember, every illegal alien is a criminal, though every criminal is not an illegal alien. The illegals cited in the stories below are a few of the really bad ones: There are lots more. These stories were publicized in 2013 when Marco Rubio was pleading for amnesty for illegals.

- **May 2013** — An illegal alien — whose identity was withheld to protect the identity of his victim — pled guilty and was convicted in Oklahoma for the statutory rape of an 11-year old child. He was sentenced to 25 years imprisonment. (KWSO Channel 7 News, May 1, 2013)
- **April 2013** — A Moroccan, Mohammed Mamdouh, was sentenced to five years imprisonment after pleading guilty in February 2012 to conspiracy to a crime of terrorism, criminal possession of a weapon and attempted possession of a weapon as a crime of terrorism in New York City. Mamdouh's fellow conspirator, Algerian Ahmed Ferhani, was sentenced to ten years imprisonment in March. (Businessweek, April 26, 2013).
- **April 2013** — Oscar Hernandez, a Mexican illegal alien was convicted in New Mexico of the murder of a woman in a fight and was sentenced to 20 years prison. (Albuquerque Jrnl; Apr 11 2013)
- **March 2013** — Angel Campos Tellez, a Mexican illegal alien, pled guilty to helping run a prostitution ring in

Maryland and Delaware. Tellez had been previously deported twice. (Washington Post, March 27, 2013)

- **March 2013** — Daniel Ignacio, a Guatemalan illegal alien, was found guilty of murder, arson and assault for torching a tenement that killed five. He faces imprisonment of 25 years to life. (*New York Times*, March 12, 2013)
- **February 2013** — Yanira del Carmen Guerrero Andrade, a Salvadoran illegal alien residing in Maryland, pled guilty to child sex trafficking for recruiting a run-away, pregnant 15-year-old into prostitution. (U.S. Department of Justice press release, Feb 13 2013)
- **January 2013** — Pereira, a Salvadoran illegal alien was sentenced to 50 years to life in prison for beating his ex-girlfriend to death in 2012 in Nebraska. (1011Now news, January 4, 2013)

I rest my case!

Tax Code -- Foreign Nationals Rip Off Americans

Is it stealing and is it criminal when a third party such as the US government steals from taxpayers to provide bonanzas to illegal foreign nationals paid for by Americans? There are two criminals in this scenario—the person receiving the bonanza (the illegal foreign national), and the person providing the bonanza (our beloved politicians). There is only one victim however—the US taxpayer— you and I.

Our lawmakers give our dollars to foreign nationals as if it is their job to give away as much of our small amount of wealth as they can. They do not throw extra in the pot from their personal stashes. Instead, they expect that you and I will pay. Some of the laws that favor illegals over Americans actually are so bad they make many Americans sick to the stomach.

You may know that the US tax code now permits dollars to be paid for child credit purposes for non-taxpayer refunds. Citizens and non-citizens, who pay no taxes at all, are eligible for huge "refunds." Our lawmakers have twisted the tax system to work as a welfare scheme for those who earn no dollars and pay no taxes and are from countries other than the USA.

They are so kind to the foreigner non-wage earners that they have chosen to include illegal aliens in the deal. Rather than deporting any illegal who files a tax return, which is required under our laws, our Congress gives most of them an extra bonus for fling a request to receive extra money from our treasury. Ask yourself, with representatives like this, would you ever give your wallet to a Congressman to hold while you bought a hit dog on the street? I know that I would not give a thief an opportunity to steal.

In April 2013, while the gang of eight tyrants were hard at work convincing Americans that we needed to treat the fifty million illegal foreign nationals even better than simply permitting them to roam free of concern from our immigration laws, illegal foreign nationals (faux Americans) were collecting real dollars in tax refunds. Our lawmakers no longer protect real Americans. Every American who has ever paid a dollar in taxes knows that this is inherently wrong.

It is time to exorcize the scum in Congress from our National monuments such as the Halls of Congress. The sooner the better. Bring in a priest or take them out at the ballot box. They gotta go.

Chapter 11 Can US Leaders Secure America from Foreigners?

Foreigners have no chance to hurt Americans when Americans believe America comes first

Please appease, please?

Most Americans are very sensitive about calling anybody names, even if they deserve it. The idea of political correctness has gone so far that many Americans are sickened by it to the point of inaction. If Vladimir Putin, for example, one day decided he did not want America to defend itself because it was an insult to the Russian people, one would almost expect the progressive PC crowd in charge of the government to ask if we might consider handing him over a few states and perhaps the full control of the oceans and space so that his ire would calm down.

Eventually, however, it is fait accompli when you seek to appease and not solve; that you run out of land and you run out of sea and the invader then wants the change you have in your pocket because he or she knows that you are so weak that you will give it up.

It would be nice to find a brave politician or diplomat in the US today who would consider America and Americans first.

Politicians are not equipped to save the day!

Have you ever met a dishonest politician? Of course, you have, if you have ever met a politician. Our dishonest politicians keep telling us that US Immigration laws are broken and we need a sort of a "comprehensive" solution to make all of us well again. But, the astute among us know that these are code words for amnesty.

We all know that the crux of the problem is the artificial constraints the Democratic Congress has placed on beds and the process for detaining migrants who overwhelm border agents. Democrats love illegal immigrants and for each one they identify, they have a pre-printed Democrat voter registration card ready to go when needed.

Congress can easily fix this problem because Congress created the problem. The facts suggest that it is actually our politicians that are broken, not our immigration laws, and we need a comprehensive cleanup to make that all OK again.

Some fumigants in their former offices would also help. Some new chairs may also be needed. If you will kindly pardon my French, my first cousin, Jimmy Brady, could say it better than any politically correct politician. Jimmy was a wise one for sure. He always reminded me that you cannot out-bull a bull-thrower. Yet, despite that indisputable fact, our government feeds us one untruth after another, hoping we will all shut-up and play nice.

Democrats play the game the best. They are naturals because they actually hate God and they hate America. This is ground we have already covered. Thank God we are Americans and the immigration game is not yet over. It is time the people won a few innings at least.

The fact is that our immigration laws per se are not broken. Our enforcement is broken. Democrats interject on asylum to hurt the enforcement at the border but that is not what the laws suggest. America is a sovereign country and we decide who comes and who does not come to America.

The additional impediments Democrats have added to the processing of detainees from Central America have made the job of border agents untenable. People of the USA, make them pay for hurting us at the ballot box in 2020 and then we can move on to solve this terrible problem at the border.

Overall, before Trump, the US Government had merely chosen that it did not wish to enforce laws made to protect the people. So, Obama and company did not enforce these laws by design. It was not an accident. It was deliberate. Then, they called it de facto amnesty as if some mythical third party did the dirty deed when they knew they did it themselves.

Democrats still have no problem lying to US. I regret to say that throwing the bums out is the best way to fix this problem and most of the other problems we face today. By electing a Democrat House, the election of November 2018 postponed a process that cannot end until the rot is fully removed from Congress. Please don't ever give Democrats any authrity over us until they actually want to help we the people.

I admit the full process is now delayed until 2020, when we have no choice but to throw out all of the Democrats and the RINOs and *Never Trumpers* left in the House. The big challenge is to find people who love America and have no major affiliation to the new Democrats so that we can all move America forward again.

How about stopping the caravan?

Mark Krikorian, who I have cited in prior chapters has a lot of great notions about how to make things better. I was influenced by him in writing this chapter.

They look like this when they are not walking. These migrants are part of a caravan of thousands from Central America on their way to a safe haven in the United States. They often hitch-hike on a truck such as this along the highway to Arriaga from Pijijiapan, Mexico.

Only Congress can fix the problem of caravan after caravan attacking our border to gain entry to the US. Congress simply does not want to do its job. RINOs want cheap labor while Socialist Democrats are looking for more and more Democrat voters.

Many Americans are asking why can't we simply stop the caravans from Central America and send them back. Why does it have to be complicated? Congress offers no excuses but they like to blame the other Party. The Democrats are responsible for all the American pain but they believe that despite the truth, Republicans and Trump will be blames. That's how stupid they are.

We all see the thousands of Central Americans making their way en-masse to the United States and so we ask ourselves "Are we willing to defend the sovereignty of our nations from invaders who want to cross our borders?"

These new invaders are not starting a *war* or are they? They have no weapons to conquer, but nevertheless they want to settle here uninvited and plunder our welfare systems. That may not be called *war* but it is awful close.

The president's threat to deploy the military to the border to stop the caravan was fulfilled for four months in 2018 until the end of January 2019. At the time, there were about 2,300 active-duty service members deployed for the border mission. This was down substantially from a height of nearly 6,000 last fall.

Defense Department officials say their work cost over $150 million, and it is on top of another $100 million spent on National Guard deployments to support border security missions last year. Just a month later, as we begin April, the caravans have started en-masse once again. Now what? Democrats, like George Carlin would have fired off meaninglessness missiles such as *"Que Passe"* or *"Not my problem, Dude."* They are right. This is a problem caused by Democrats and they definitely do not want to solve it any time soon.

This is not really a military problem but maybe it is. It is definitely a law-enforcement problem. However, ordinary civilian law enforcement does not have the tools and in some cases, the will power (sanctuaries) to solve the problem.

The current rules pushed by Congress regarding asylum and the treatment of alien minors, and the inadequate level of funding for detention of people applying for asylum (to make sure they can't run off when their cases are rejected), effectively force border agents and others engaged in the battle into what is called *a catch-and-release policy.*

I cannot believe I composed such a large sentence as the one above. This is just stupid so ask Congress why it is so. Aliens crossing the border are given a court date and then let go in the US. Real Americans know that this is a powerful incentive for more people to follow from Central America. We might suggest that it is not just an incentive, it is a personal invitation.

Though the massive caravans that occur sporadically do present a highly photogenic part of the problem; looking back to 2018, we see statistics that show there was a less obvious slow-motion caravan confronting the border every single day. For example, a daily average in September 2018 of more than 500 illegal aliens traveling in family units were apprehended on the border—then contrary to common sense were soon released.

It is too easy and it would be just as easy to shut down if our Congress was not loaded with Democrats and RINOS who like it the way it is. Can you imagine?

These people have been instructed to simply walk up to an immigration inspector at a legal crossing point on the Mexican border ("port of entry" is the technical term) and utter the magic word "asylum." This gets them in and they need no monopoly money to pull off this trick. Name a Democrat you know who probably gave these interlopers the magic words. Don't say *George Soros* because for all we know, he is so old, unlike Joe Biden, he is probably dead. Haina?

So, what should we Americans do with an ineffective Congress and a real emergency facing us. Trump may very well close the border and this would be a good start even though the guacamole might disappear for a few months. Our country is at stake so let's figure out how California can again be the Guacamole State.

Bring on the border troops

Euphemistically, throwing troops at the problem will not do any lasting good because they can't arrest people and just like in the fall of 2018 there would be a clamor for the NG troops to be released back to their home towns. Moms and kids do not care about border security when Dad, a stock broker or something else is tied up not providing every day victuals for sustenance.

It is tough for troops to solve anything anyway. They're obviously not going to open fire on unarmed people. Even land mines and machine guns atop concrete border walls wouldn't matter much, since most of those arriving would simply go to a legal port of entry.

It is almost futile because Congress actually fights good border enforcement when it is proposed. And, so, as much as one-third of last spring's caravan actually made it all the way to the border, and of those, the large majority went to ports of entry. If Congress cared, this could all be shut down and only those we want in the country would be admitted. Should Americans decide how many and actually, who should have a right to gain access to America?

Most Americans would prefer that we offer family reunification in the home country like Guatemala, not in the United States. The governments of South American countries are not ready to deal with their own issues. It would be good to have a small Peace Corps-like force of US business people working in these countries to assure the leaders do not steal US money intended to make living better for the rest.

Better than cash, the new US corps could build shelters and help in farming and manufacturing and whatever would help the people of the country that instead chooses to send its people to our borders

Giving the leaders cash has not done it for the US even though it is very altruistic and overall a good idea. It just has not worked and must be improved.

So, the President's threat to cut off foreign aid to the source and transit countries south of the border is not fanciful and it is not counterproductive. Money talks. The whole point of that money is to reduce emigration pressures, so eliminating it to do-gooders might seem like cutting off your nose to spite your face. But it is a better deal for those in need.

Some have suggested that if the aid isn't doing any good, we should just cut it off, caravan or no caravan, rather than using it as a threat. I disagree. We should investigate and learn why things go wrong with so much money and we should correct them after shutting off the spigot. US analysts and auditors can determine the cause and recommend a solution without continuing to pay for nothing in any country not willing to participate. A wasted dollar is a wasted dollar.

Another recent suggestion of the President's is his threat to shut down the border. This is a very realistic way to pressure Mexico to stop the caravan. It is not without precedent as President Nixon did essentially the same thing back in 1969 to pressure Mexico on drugs. President Reagan did the same in 1985 when the Mexicans became recalcitrant during the investigation re the kidnapping of DEA agent Kiki Camarena.

Another less draconian solution—though I think draconian solutions do show we mean business and are not to be taken lightly would be to use the shutdown tool as needed. For example, if some large share of a caravan descends upon a single port of entry, we can close that one. We have to put up with a bit of economic distress in order to make a big point with the goal of solving the problem. Even though our economy may be more integrated with Mexico's than it was in the 1960 or even the 1980s, the pain would still be significantly greater for Mexico than the US and this is a big issue that must be solved. New solutions will bring other innovative approaches to change the Mexican will to be helpful rather than hurtful.

Why not deputize state and local law enforcement to make immigration arrests (which the law permits in the case of "an actual or imminent mass influx of aliens arriving off the coast of the United States, or near a land border"). Why not set up emergency tent-city detention centers on the border? How about using the travel-ban authority to prohibit the admission of anyone participating in a caravan? With no action, there will be no movement from this Congress to be innovative. It is time for action.

We don't see all of DHS's Nielson's plans and presentations but she is on our side for sure. All these ideas and more may already be included in the existing contingency plans for coping with a "Mass Immigration Emergency." The president could declare appropriate action if the caravan reaches our border with the kinds of numbers we're seeing in southern Mexico.

Of course, the President and the Executive Branch cannot do it alone. Congress cannot continue to thwart fair minded notions to solve the problem. Most agree that the big problem that can be fixed quickly by Congress is an overly permissive asylum system (including rules for dealing with illegal-alien minors). We know that this invites more and more foreign national interlopers into the country. Moreover, it is now the preferred way to penetrate our borders for those with no other way to do so. Only Congress can fix that but so far the Democrats seem to like Americans and border agents to suffer while they entice new Democrat voters to jump the border.

By forcing Mexico to stop the caravans before they get to our border, or even declaring a Mass Immigration Emergency, congressional Democrats , who hold most of the blame, get left off the hook. Given the persistence of the filibuster rule requiring a supermajority for the passage of any legislation to plug border leaks (like the Flores agreement and the Trafficking Victims Protection Reauthorization Act —both regarding minors — and low standards for establishing the "credible fear" needed to justify asylum) or to increase detention capacity, Chuck Schumer and his Democrat coterie have an effective veto over efforts to enforce the border. Schumer needs to be taken out to the woodshed on this – figuratively but many would like to see it done literally.

The people of the US cannot stand by, regardless of which Party you are from. As Americans we have a right to exert political pressure on Democratic lawmakers, through letters to the editor and letters to Congress and rallies—not just through White House statements. Reluctant wimpish Republicans are not off the hook either. Their leadership in Congress must force them to vote on targeted measures addressing specific vulnerabilities. It may be impossible to get the 4th Estate (the press) to do its job but it sure is time. What side are they on?

A longer-term plan is also needed. I've got a great plan that deals with the 60 million illegal interloper residents in the country today. You'll see it in some of my other books from 2018. As border control improves and we (hopefully) do a better job of policing legal visitors to ensure their timely departure, bogus claims of asylum will continue to become the primary way to circumvent immigration limits. Congress is the blame for this and the people must replace the greedy with the caring. If you don't love America, don't run for Congress.

Another concept that must be operationalized both in statute and through bilateral agreements is "safe third country." The 1967 Protocol Relating to the Status of Refugees, the U.N. treaty that governs these matters, says states must recognize the refugee status of aliens "coming directly from a territory where their life or freedom was threatened."

People who pass through other countries with asylum systems (such as Mexico) should not be permitted even to apply for asylum because they are, by definition, no longer fleeing persecution. If Democrats would only represent the US instead of foreign interests, using this idea would be a real help for the control of immigration to the US. Come on Congress, do your jobs before we have to replace you all.

There are lot of other notions. Another long-term objective should be to limit the grounds for asylum. Currently the U.N. language, incorporated into the 1980 Refugee Act, says asylum is for those persecuted because of their "race, religion, nationality, membership of a particular social group or political opinion." It is the fourth of these five categories that has been the source of much mischief; "membership in a particular social group" is a catch-all that activist lawyers and their judicial accomplices have used to try to pry open our borders, concocting non-existent "groups" as a way of finagling asylum. We can make the language more precise.

As Justice Samuel Alito wrote when he was still a circuit-court judge, "read in its broadest literal sense, the phrase is almost completely open-ended. Virtually any set including more than one person could be described as a 'particular social group.'" The attorney general is instructing immigration judges to interpret the term narrowly, but only excising it from the law altogether can prevent its use by the opponents of borders. We can do it if Congress works for Americans first.

The fact is that the U.N. treaty mandates "particular social group" as a basis for asylum. For that reason, and more generally to reassert control over who is allowed into our country, the president should withdraw from the treaty. When NAFTA did not serve the US, the President got us out. So also, with this UN treaty. It is not working for America.

Accepting this defacto, as it stands now, we have created a "right" to asylum in the United States. We have in essence surrendered our sovereignty and the consequences of a disloyal Congress are becoming increasingly clear. Only the American people, through their elected representatives, (Yes, our distracted members of Congress) should decide who gets to move here, not individual foreigners asserting a "right" created by the U.N. and vindicated by post-national anti-borders activists.

You might consider additional reading and the subtitle of John Fonte's 2011 book poses the first question we all must ask ourselves as we assess the US asylum policy: "Will Americans Rule Themselves or Be Ruled by Others?" I say, America first, last, and all-ways.

Broken pieces brought first to US by Obama

Americans who can still think know that the biggest chunks of the broken pieces of the puzzle is the American political system and the federal government's control of immigration. Other than the asylum notion, the laws are not bad. The enforcement, however, is not worthy of the Constitution.

Why do Americans have to put up with a group of bureaucrats who feel it is OK to publicly state that it is OK that they not do their jobs, among which is border enforcement and shipping the invaders home. We get a chance to send the bums (Congress) home on a regular basis. This next time, for the good of the country, we must clean our House.

Is it not an atrocity when God-fearing Americans elect corrupt / pandering / lawless politicians who put party, lobbyist, & self-interest ahead of the Constitution of our USA and the rule of law? It may be easy to accept this in good times, but these times are really tough. With the politicians in charge, you can bet things are not going to get any better any time soon.

Suppose the US Congress were able to ram through an amnesty bill to "solve the ills of the country." It would look just like the McCain / Schumer / Rubio bill fashioned by the gang of eight tyrants. The proposed immigration amnesty would surely benefit the 60 or more million illegal foreign nationals (illegal aliens) who are currently living in the United States, but it would hurt Americans and future prospects for employment and a decent wage in ways unimaginable. And, it would bankrupt the country. Let Democrats put their own wallets up as collateral if this is what they want and I bet they shut up quickly if conservative wallets are not in the mix.

An amnesty program for illegal aliens forgives their acts of illegal aggression and implicitly forgives other related illegal acts such as illegal driving and working with false documents. It also tells others back in the home nations to come on down!

The result of an amnesty is that large numbers of foreign nationals, who illegally gain entry into the United States, are rewarded with legal status, green card, or the grand prize, American citizenship for breaking the line while breaking US immigration laws. It is not fair to Americans, in-line citizen aspirants, and it is simply not right.

President Barack Obama was a broken record often stating that "we are not going to ship back 12 million people." Note that the President used the number 12 million though he knew it was 60 million. He lied regularly to the people so this exaggeration was expected. Sometimes he used his own mouth to lie and other times, as Darryl Issa notes, he uses his paid liar, Press Secretary Carney to lie for him.

Regarding deportation, Obama said; "we're not going to do it as a practical matter. We would have to take all our law enforcement that we have available and we would have to use it and put people on buses, and rip families apart, and that's not who we are, that's not what America is about." What a bunch of bunk!.

What would it cost to deport illegal aliens?

Is the President correct that we cannot afford to ship people back? Was the President right on many matters over his eight years? Did President Obama really believe that this poor hapless country called the United States that fought countless wars to keep its freedoms, all of sudden could not protect its own borders from potential aggressors? With him as commander in chief, this was true because he did not have the will.

This country somehow was able to put the first man on the moon and through its exceptionalism has become the most powerful nation on earth. We can do anything we choose and Obama could have made the right thing happen. As president, he declined. We are America, the strongest nation on earth. We control our own destiny.

Before the end of the 1960's while other countries were still trying to accomplish more simple endeavors, such as perfecting moonshine, the US was on to one-of-a-kind major accomplishments. The Southern US had already perfected moonshine so we had plenty of time to get real things done.

Let's not forget that President Kennedy, a person, who loved America and Americans, toasted heartily the work of Neil Armstrong after his moon walk in June 1969, months ahead of schedule. Can it be that Obama was kidding about America not having the will or the capability to deport 60,000,000 aliens? I do not doubt that this past president did not have the will and he copped out on helping Americans fight illegal foreign nationals.

Is it enough for our leaders to decry their own failings by calling this perpetration de facto amnesty when instead it was de facto incompetence? While I am at it, let me state for the record that the US is a great country and we surely have what it takes to fix our border problem at the same time. We just need the corrupt Democrats to get out of our way.

The Country needs our help

When Charles E. Weller was looking for a good typing drill, he chose the sentence, "Now is the time for all good men to come to the aid of the party" His phrase was picked up by many typing books. However, over time, the phrase was improved to the variant "Now is the time for all good men to come to the aid of their country."

Weller's practice line happens to exactly fill out a 70-space line if you put a period at the end so it is perfect for typing school. I would like to suggest that if we use the older use of "men" to mean "a human regardless of sex or age," the term is also perfect to describe what all citizens of the United States must now do to protect our country from being overwhelmed by illegal foreign nationals.

Say no to the Rubio / Schumer gang of eight tyrants' and their long-defeated 2013 immigration reform plan. Say no to any reincarnation of this plan. Say not to Democrat insistence that there is no border emergency when we know all they want is more Democrat voters.

The amnesty bill would have taken America down. Let's repeat the typing jingle one more time and type it if we must to remember it well in this, the second decade of the new millennium: "Now is the time for all good men to come to the aid of their country." Thank you. Are you ready to afford deportation and the protection of our southern border from invaders? I think we all are.

Chapter 12 What if Somebody Broke Into Your House?

Southwestern states are hurt the most!

Yes, government lies, continues to lie, and enjoys lying because low information Americans, mostly Democrats believe their lies, and feel better about them possibly being the truth. California, Arizona, New Mexico, and Texas, are the four states most affected by the bulk of illegal foreign nationals who most often cross our southern border. As we examine a similar threat on the northern border, we must take into consideration a means to solve that problem at the same time.

While thinking about what must be done to help illegal aliens, ask yourself this question: "If somebody broke into your house tonight while you are out with the family at a restaurant celebrating a family birthday, and when you got home they were stuffing their faces on your Sunday prior leftovers and perhaps they got some good stuff out of the freezer, cooked it up along with some wine, some good drinks, etc., would you ask them what you should do to help them further?" Would you go out and get them dessert? I don't think so!

Would you tell them where the rest of your good stuff is? Or would you tell them to get the hell out? I rest my case. Americans owe illegal interlopers nothing. However, because we have been so dumb to allow greedy politicians to condone this crap since 1986, the last amnesty, perhaps we can do well by Americans and do OK by the interlopers by changing the rules.

The term illegal immigration has come to evoke images of hapless people eluding US authorities at the border, yet more and more of those in the US illegally come on tourist, student, religious and work visas. When their visa expires, they simply choose to stay. It is a no brainer. If they choose not to go home, they simply stay since America chooses not to track their whereabouts while they are in the US. BTW, isn't that a shame?

So, no matter how good we get at securing both borders, and we have to become almost perfect at that, we cannot discount the huge number of illegal residents that come from the six million or more visas that the US grants each and every year to people we have not vetted. Why should they ever go home when the border jumpers will testify that the toughest part of living in America is getting here? If you are already here, you are well more than 90% of the way to never having to go home.

That is how dumb US authorities actually have become. Actually, with liberal / progressive communists in charge of the government, perhaps replacing current citizens with like-minded statists is a good idea for the Emperor.

Visas are often unlawfully extended

An H-1B work visa, for example, is just one type of many visas by which legal foreign nationals are permitted to work in the US for up to six years. After six years, with an H-1B, the former legal alien, by law, is supposed to go home. But, many American officials, right up to the Obama White House when he was CEO of America do not care about the laws they are sworn to uphold.

So, many with expired visas, choose not to go home ever. They simply stay. They continue to work for the company that sponsored them originally. They are not dumb. They choose to stay illegal in America since Obama had told them implicitly that it was really OK unless they are criminals. The company continues to pay them as if all is copacetic. Nobody even chastises the company. Why? To repeat the answer, and it is very simple—Democrats want new Democrat voters and Republicans want cheap labor. What chance do the people have against all that power. That is why Trump got elected.

Why say no?

Unfortunately, US officials have simply given up on tracking expired visa holders. Only in government work, is the response "I can't" acceptable. In all jobs I have had in my career, if something is not in your job description, you tend to let it slide—knowing you are ultimately accountable but hoping to solve immediate crises and then get back to that issue left behind.

Perhaps there are benefits for the would-be enforcers to choose not to enforce? Why don't we know this? We in the US reap what we sew from planting poor politicians in our fields. Why we cannot know who has arrived and who has left is a primitive IT problem that a freshman IT major could solve even before the first semester is over.

We can send astronauts to the moon and repair space stations in space but US officials are convinced that we cannot track a few million non-Americans. I disagree. First, they must register with biometrics and full demographics. Then, they would be in some database someplace, and they would be fully track-able. There should be no way that any interloper, once registered, could be lost. I implicitly trust IBM, my former employer, and its methods and I know that if the US actually wanted a good system that was impregnable, IBM could deliver it. I would be tickled to temporarily help the country them free of charge!

Not being able to find interlopers is sheer government incompetence. As a professional IT expert, I could ask a freshman IT class at the university to design a system over one or two semesters that would be able to assure that visa holders behave exactly as they are supposed to, including leaving the country on time. Americans are pretty smart. American officials unfortunately are not! Actually, maybe they are as the default is more Democrat voters and cheap labor and that is exactly what our elected officials want.

Many Americans have not learned yet that the Obama Administration had relaxed all border crossings from Mexico and Canada for the last several years. The border agents and the field personnel find this as strange as do regular Americans. But, then again, like most of US, they do not have an "in" to the back of the Obama brain. It is as if the past President was interested in telegraphing a means to illegally enter to the enemy. Your call, not mine! Trump thinks like we do but our corrupt cowardly Congress is fighting him

Canada and the US once had superior security. One-time years ago, for example, I took my two young sons to Canada on a special Dad trip. They were less than ten years old each and very little. At the border, when passports were not required, we were all detained for an inordinate amount of time. My children were separated from me on our way into Canada. US border officials wanted to make sure I was not kidnapping my children. I was OK with that.

In their thirties now, my boys still have a lot of moxie and chicanery, and I thought their miniature versions back then might try to trick the authorities into thinking that they were being hustled across the border by a dad to avoid mom's bad dinners and lunches. (Sorry Pat – just kidding). In the end, I was thankful for the work of the border guards, as border checks would surely limit illicit transportation activities between the two countries. If my sons were ever kidnapped, I would love the opportunity to scoot to the border to retrieve these wonderful, highly-loved small people when they were returned. Why would Obama want to change that?

Secure the Border

Americans say, "Secure the border first." Border fortification is the most important notion in any "comprehensive plan." Most Americans do not trust that the gang of eight tyrants will ever secure the border, regardless of their promises. In the Kelly comprehensible plan, border security must be achieved. No more interlopers are permitted under any circumstances. We should be able to do perfectly well with the illegal population that is already here. Thus, no additional immigrants will be permitted until we believe we need them. Once we prove those in the country are OK, we can figure out what additional people we need. I think we need none. Only those wishing to pay $2.00 or less per hour would think otherwise. And, this is not 1965!

Chapter 13 An EMAIL That Haunts the Senses

Sometimes the Inbox has the secret solution

Don't you love getting an email that you know is special—that spells out something you have been trying to say when you just cannot find the words. In this book, I use over 45,000 words to leave my message of hope for Americans if only we can curb the wrongheadedness of our Democrat pro-amnesty friends. No amnesty and no way.

I like this email from the La Bonte family so much that I will also leave it with you. If you have read this before from your inbox, you can almost pack it in now, as you have completed most of this book. Feel free to check out other books by Brian Kelly.

I hope this email haunts you as much as it haunts me. I prefix it with a few of the original annoying headers that came with it:

X-Received: by 10.49.95.231 with SMTP id
dn7mr23736074qeb.63.1381510501484;
Mon, 17 Jun 2013 16:08:21 -0700 (PDT)
Authentication-Results: mx.google.com;   spf=pass (google.com:
domain of rudy@aol.com designates 64.12.144.86 as permitted
sender)
From: "Rudy"
Subject: New Immigrants
Date: Mon, 17 Jun 2013 19:08:08 -0400
X-Mailer: Microsoft Outlook 14.0

"New Immigrants" is the subject. This is a very good letter to the editor. This woman made some good points. For some reason, people have difficulty structuring their arguments when arguing against supporting the currently proposed immigration revisions. This lady made the argument pretty simple. This was <u>NOT</u> printed in the Orange County Paper...................

Newspapers simply won't publish letters to the editor which they either deem politically incorrect (read below) or which do not agree with the philosophy the paper has pushed on the public. This woman wrote a great letter to the editor that should have been published; but, with your help it will get published forever via cyberspace!

From: "David LaBonte"

My wife, Rosemary, wrote a wonderful letter to the editor of the OC Register which, of course, was not printed. So, I decided to "print" it myself by sending it out on the Internet. Pass it along if you feel so inclined. Written in response to a series of letters to the editor in the Orange County Register:

Dear Editor:
So many letter writers have based their arguments on how this land is made up of immigrants. Ernie Lujan for one, suggests we should tear down the Statue of Liberty because the people now in question aren't being treated the same as those who passed through Ellis Island and other ports of entry.

Maybe we should turn to our history books and point out to people like Mr. Lujan why today's American is not willing to accept this new kind of immigrant any longer. Back in 1900 when there was a rush from all areas of Europe to come to the United States, people had to get off a ship and stand in a long line in New York and be documented. Some would even get down on their hands and knees and kiss the ground. They made a pledge to uphold the laws and support their new country in good and bad times. They made learning English a primary rule in their new American households and some even changed their names to blend in with their new home.

They had waved good bye to their birth place to give their children a new life and did everything in their power to help their children assimilate into one culture. Nothing was handed to them. No free lunches, no welfare, no labor laws to protect them. All they had were the skills and craftsmanship they had brought with them to trade for a future of prosperity.

Most of their children came of age when World War II broke out. My father fought alongside men whose parents had come straight over from Germany, Italy, France and Japan. None of these 1st generation Americans ever gave any thought about what country their parents had come from. They were Americans fighting Hitler, Mussolini and the Emperor of Japan. They were defending the United States of America as one people.

When we liberated France, no one in those villages were looking for the French-American or the German American or the Irish American. The people of France saw only Americans. And we carried one flag that represented one country. Not one of those immigrant sons would have thought about picking up another country's flag and waving it to represent who they were. It would have been a disgrace to their parents who had sacrificed so much to be here. These immigrants truly knew what it meant to be an American. They stirred the melting pot into one red, white and blue bowl.

And here we are with a new kind of immigrant who wants the same rights and privileges. Only they want to achieve it by playing with a different set of rules, one that includes the entitlement card and a guarantee of being faithful to their mother country. I'm sorry, that's not what being an American is all about. I believe that the immigrants who landed on Ellis Island in the early 1900's deserve better than that for all the toil, hard work and sacrifice in raising future generations to create a land that has become a beacon for those legally searching for a better life.

I think they would be appalled that they are being used as an example by those waving foreign country flags.

And for that suggestion about taking down the Statue of Liberty, it happens to mean a lot to the citizens who are voting on the immigration bill. I wouldn't start talking about dismantling the United States just yet.

(It was signed when written)
Rosemary LaBonte

Chapter 14 Build the Wall to Stop Migrant Caravans

This Getty Image shows Migrants attempting to cross the border fence to the United States at Playa de Tijuana, Mexico.

Democrats care about New Voters; not helping the impoverished.

 The facts and some opinion in this chapter come mostly from the New York Post, a paper whose roots go back to Alexander Hamilton. Most of the information for this chapter is from a work by John Crudele published on January 16, 2019 https://nypost.com/2019/01/16/we-need-to-build-the-border-wall-to-stop-the-migrant-caravans/

The recent Democrat posture on the wall is new and it has two purposes.

1. To deny Trump any political victory over the D congress
2. Democrat were never against illegal immigration – they want more Democrats.

Two faced Democrats want the public to believe they are for border security when they are not. Remember that Democrats voted against the safety of Americans in 2019. Remember that next time you vote.

When the government shut-down was in place, John Crudele, who wrote much of the based-on article for the Post, changed his mind about building a wall along the Mexican border. He now says, "Build it!" Unless you are dishonest and have a political reason or you simply hate Trump, you've got to be for a wall to protect US sovereignty and protect the country.

The US government was shut down during the last part of December and January 2019 and the economic ramifications were not insignificant. Not only were the families of people who've been put out of work being hurt, but the entire economy could have been affected. Trump had already boosted the economy sufficiently enough that it could have withstood months of a shutdown but the Democrat-loving press would never report that.

Like most Americans, Crudele did not like the shutdown because grown men in Congress paid to do the right thing were acting like babies. Some of us liked the shutdown for one reason and that was that it might make both sides reconsider their positions and go ahead and build the wall. The country needs the wall.

The research of a Chicago-based global outplacement & career transitioning firm, concluded that the shutdown could reduce consumer spending by $3.4 billion a month. And since the consumer is the biggest part of our economy, that was expected to hurt regular people besides the government workers who were not getting paid while working. That's a part of the reason Crudele did not like the shutdown.

There were a lot of hard-heads stuck to the shoulders of the politicians in Washington. The President and conservatives wanted agreement on the wall and he used the budget as a means of getting funding. Nany Pelosi and Chuck Schumer, both of whom had just several years ago been for a wall, said there would be no wall. Both sides were fixed in their positions and the government was standing still and shut down.

Amidst these two immovable objects, that's when John Crudele decided to change his mind about the wall. He's right.

Crudele says his long-held position on immigration is simple: Immigrants are necessary. In fact, they are vitally important if the economy is going to continue to grow and if we want the budget deficit to go down and Social Security to be saved. America's population just isn't growing fast enough to maintain a vibrant economy.

Crudele says that demographics are working against us—too many people are going into retirement age (when less is spent, less paid in taxes and more Social Security payments are handed out) and there aren't enough people taking their places as workers and taxpayers. So, we need immigration. The more the better, in fact— xcept that we need people who will become employed and be the solutions to our problems and not add to the problems. We need workers, not freeloaders. That is the Crudele position. IMHO, it is too simple.

I did not get to talk to Crudele. So why did he change his mind about the wall? That answer is simple: "Because of the caravans of immigrants assaulting our southern border."

Crudele posits that building a wall just for a relative trickle of immigrants who've been crossing the border for decades would have been expensive overkill at a time when the US should have been watching its spending. He figured there should be more cost-effective, high-tech ways to catch small groups of illegal intruders.

Now that huge "caravans" of people wanting to become illegal foreign nationals in our country are trying to enter the US from the south, the wall makes a whole lot more sense. In fact, Crudele believes that "Trump couldn't have asked for a better excuse for his beloved barricade." I, your humble author believe the wall is necessary in order for America to remain a sovereign country with the American people in charge and not the rich Democrat or Republican donors who want to call all the shots.

Crudele talks about the past, in which there had been "caravans" of sorts coming into the US. He admits these were ships and were not endless funnels of humanity coming from South America and Mexico. Immigrants coming from Europe in droves technically came by floating caravans. But the difference was that when they arrived here, they were screened and allowed to stay if they were deemed not to become a burden on the social services system. People with major diseases were turned around in Ellis Island and sent back home for free at the expense of the steamship captains that brought them.

Today's "migrants are hell bent on living in America regardless of the opinions of the citizens of the United States. They seem to believe they are entitled to a free ride in America."

Crudele makes a good point when he says that "If people want to come from Latin America to the US, either by caravan or some other way, then they should undergo the same rigorous testing as those people in the ship caravans. They should come here legally!"

Here's another piece of what he thinks: "Our politicians are acting like babies. Trump wants what he wants. And the Democrats have suddenly shifted their views on border security just to annoy the president and in hope that it gets him out of office in 2020." Perfecto Mr. Crudele.

This is not about offering a better life for the impoverished from the southern hemisphere. If it were the Dems would have accepted one of the many deals to legalize the "Dreamers" put forth by Republicans to get the wall built. The Democrats simply want to embarrass Trump and of course they want as many illegals as possible to populate the country so that they can gain more Democrat voters.

Looking back to a June 24, 2013, article in the New York Times, you can gain a lot of insight into the chicanery involved in the "border fight if you don't believe either Crudele or me.

The headline is *"Senate Vote on Border Gives Push to Immigration Overhaul."* Barack Obama, a Democrat, was president at that time. Democrats controlled the Senate back then, Republicans controlled the House.

With the war between Democrats and the Republicans with Democrats trying to impeach Trump every day, neither Party is helping the people They should be more concerned about another kind of threat. John Kelly, Trump's former chief of staff, once said in an interview that the threat of terrorism from across the Mexican border "keeps me literally awake at night…"We know that would be the Super Bowl for the terrorists to knock down an airplane in flight," Kelly said on "Face the Nation" on April 23, 2017.

The truth is that American intelligence agencies are afraid that terrorists have already snuck high-powered weapons across the Mexican border through tunnels. There are many details that DHS and the intelligence communities have that they cannot share here.

Politicians on both sides of the wall are going to look very stupid if there is a big terrorist strike because of something that came through Mexico. In the meantime, cut a deal. Crudele's message and my message is "Build the wall!"

Chapter 15 Immigrants Were Checked out at Ellis Island

The medical examination at Ellis Island

Though Democrats and the press like to deny there is any connection with the recent outbreak of measles and other once-eradicated diseases in the United States. Perhaps this health warning from Tijuana Mexico in November gives us some insights. Would Democrats and the press lie about this if they thought it would turn the people against their plan for more and more illegal aliens in line to be Democrat voters?

"Migrants who came with the caravan are suffering from respiratory infections, tuberculosis, chickenpox and other serious health issues, Tijuana's Health Department warned on Thursday morning."

The press does not talk much about the diseases that illegal immigrants who have not had medical examinations bring with them to the country. They are not checked and not vetted and it is a safety risk for Americans. Besides diseases, the "migrants" are illegal and a source for criminals and terrorists to enter the country.

Ellis Island made sure America and Americans were safe

http://www.ellisisland.se/english/ellisisland_immigration3.asp

Ellis Island was not a treat for immigrants for sure but they did it and that was part of coming to America legally. The following paragraphs describe the process at Ellis Island used to check the worthiness of an aspirant for residence in the United States at the turn of the last century.

After entering the main building, immigrants left their luggage below and were guided up to the second floor, to the Registry Room. The immigrants were unaware that their journey up the steps was actually part of the health inspection

From the first steps on the stairs up to second floor every immigrant was inspected by the doctors. The doctors viewed them from above to watch for weakness, heavy breathing (indication of heart problems) and any signs of mental disturbances.

When every immigrant passed, the doctor with the help of an interpreter, examined the hair, face, neck and hands of every person. The doctor had a chalk in his hand, when he noticed that some area needed to be checked more thoroughly, he wrote a letter directly on the immigrant's clothes. About 2 of 10 persons got a letter on their clothes. This check became known as "the six second physicals".

Here is what the letters meant:

X - high up at the frontside of right shoulder - mental defects.
X - further down on the right shoulder - disease or deformity.
X - within a circle - some definite disease.
B - back problems
G - struma
H - heart problems
Pg - pregnancy
Ct - eye disease

The next doctor was the "Eye doctor"

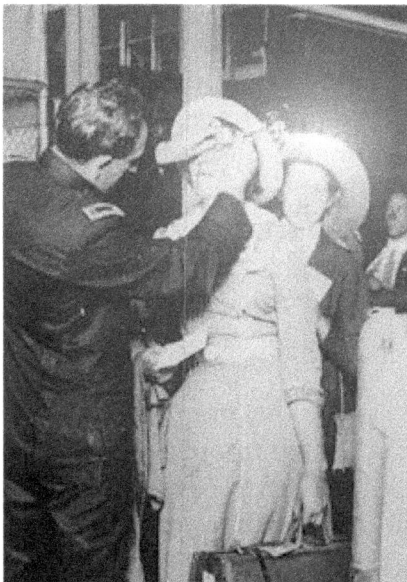

These doctors searched for a disease in the eyes called trachoma. This eye disease cause blindness and it could also lead to death. Today it is easily treated. Nearly 50% of those who had to be examined further before registration was due to this eye disease. The immigrant was mark with the letters Ct. If the doctors later on could determine the diagnosis trachoma the immigrant was sent back home at the steamship operator's expense.

If they had other diseases and these were confirmed or if the immigrant was too sick and too weak to manage to work, they were not allowed to enter to the US. They too were sent back at the steamship operator's expense.

Sick children from 12 years old or older were sent back by themselves to their home harbor. Children under 12 years old that were not allowed to stay in the US were forced to go back with one parent. Many tears were dropped when the parents should decide which parent that should stay and which parent that should go back with the sick child. It's the way it was. The inspections were intended to help citizens, not immigrants.

Interrogation

After the check-up by the doctor the immigrant went on to a long queue (waiting line) were they waited for the interrogation. In the Registry Room, approximately 5,000 people would be waiting at the same time.

The inspectors were in the front of the line. After waiting in the queue, the immigrants went forward one by one to the inspector who sat far front in the Registry Room on a high chair behind his desk. Beside himself he had an interpreter and in front he had the ship lists.

The check-up was regarding the information that the immigrant had left of himself and that was also written in the ship records. Here they double checked the name, age, religion, last residence, sex, civil status and if the immigrant should meet up with some relative etc. They spent no more than 2 minutes with every immigrant

Every inspector had just 2 minutes of time to use per immigrant to determine that the information was correct and that the person could take care of himself and fulfil the demands to be able to stay in the US. They would also determine if the person was a danger to the society. Due to that the short time frame to do this check-up, it could happen that the spelling of their name could be wrong (this was not common though). Sometimes even the home country would be wrong.

If there were any reservations about the OK-ness, the immigrant had to stay at Ellis Island for further investigation.

When Approved!

Most immigrants passed the interrogation and got their "landing card" (the permit to leave and enter New York). Only 2% of all the immigrants who went to America had to return to their home country after the check-up at Ellis Island. They returned on a steamship at the owner's expense.

After approval they only had a few hours left on Ellis Island, before they could leave the island and continue their travel.

To leave Ellis Island

After approval it was time to leave the island and continue to the final destination.

Change money

Those who had received their permission to enter to the US continued to the Money Exchange at the island. Here you could change gold, silver and foreign currency to American Dollars. Here money from all countries were exchanged to American dollars. The day´s official rates applied and those were written on a black board.

Tickets

For those who needed to travel further to cities outside New York, they had to obtain train tickets. Trains were the major transportation then. The tickets were bought at the island. At the island, there were dozens of agencies from different railway offices that sold tickets.

Sometimes as many as 25 tickets were sold in a minute when the most people were gathered.

The immigrant waited on the island at the spot for the specific railway agency (a marked area) who then took them on the ferry to the railway station.

There were several railway stations depending on destination. Railway stations could be found in Jersey City and Hoboken. Immigrants that needed to travel further to New England took the ferry to Manhattan.

The luggage - not to forget!

When everything was okay for their departure from Ellis Island, their luggage was given back to them. In the luggage the immigrant had everything from their home country—everything they loved and treasured and could carry.

The time at Ellis Island is over

With their landing card, American money, train tickets, luggage and lunchbox, the immigrants were ready to leave Ellis Island and were prepared to deal with their new destinations. For most people the trip had started several months or years earlier and still they had a long way to travel within the US, maybe to Chicago, Minnesota, Montana or the whole way to California.

Welcome to America!

Immigrants were then off to their destinations

Doesn't it make you wonder why our parents and parent's parents were so concerned about checking out all immigrants while today's Democrats want to accept them all, legal and illegal without any checking. Why do you think that is?

LETS GO PUBLISH! Books by Brian Kelly:
(Amazon.com, and Kindle)

Hope for Wilkes-Barre—John Q. Doe—Next Mayor of Wilkes-Barre *The John Doe Plan, for a better city!*
The Cowardly Congress Whatever happened to Congress doing the work of the people?
Help for Mayor George and Next Mayor of Wilkes-Barre How to vote for the next Mayor Council abbreviated
Ghost of Wilkes-Barre Future: Spirit's advice for residents about how to pick the next Mayor and Council
Great Players in Air Force Football: Air Force's best players of all time
Great Coaches in Air Force Football: From Coach 1 to Coach Troy Calhoun
Great Moments in Air Force Football: From day 1 to today!
Great Players in Navy Football: Navy's best including Bellino & Staubach
Great Coaches in Navy Football: From Coach 1 to Coach #39 Ken Niumatalolo
Great Moments in Navy Football: From day 1 to coach Ken Niumatalolo l
No Tree! No Toys! No Toot! Heartwarming story. Christmas gone while 19 month old napped
How to End DACA, Sanctuary Cities, & Resident Illegal Aliens . best solution to wipe shadows in America.
Government Must Stop Ripping Off Seniors' Social Security!: Hey buddy, seniors can no longer spare a dime?
Special Report: Solving America's Student Debt Crisis!: The only real solution to the $1.52 Trillion debt
How to End DACA, Sanctuary Cities, & Resident Illegal Aliens . best solution to wipe shadows in America.
The Winning Political Platform for America Unique winning approach to solve the big problems in America.
Lou Barletta v Bob Casey for US Senate Barletta's unique approach to solving the big problems in America.
John Chrin v Matt Cartwright for Congress Chrin has a unique approach to solving big problems in America.
The Cure for Hate !!! Can the cure be any worse than this disease that is crippling America?
Andrew Cuomo's Time to Go? "He Was Never that Great!": Cuomo says America never that great
White People Are Bad! Bad! Bad! Whoever thought a popular slogan in 2018 would be *It's OK to be White!*
The Fake News Media Is Also Corrupt !!!: Fake press / media today is not worthy to be 4th Estate.
God Gave US Donald Trump?   Trump was sent from God as the people's answer
Millennials Say America Was "Never That Great": Too many pleased days of political chumps not over!
White People Are Bad! Bad! Bad! In 2018, too many people find race as a non-equalizer.
It's Time for The John Q. Doe Party… Don't you think? By Elephants.
Great Players in Florida Gators Football… Tim Tebow and a ton of other great players
Great Coaches in Florida Gators Football… The best coaches in Gator history.
The Constitution by Hamilton, Jefferson, Madison, et al. The Real Constitution
The Constitution Companion. Will help you learn and understand the Constitution
Great Coaches in Clemson Football The best Clemson Coaches right to Dabo Swinney
Great Players in Clemson Football The best Clemson players in history
Winning Back America. America's been stolen and can be won back completely
The Founding of America… Great book to pick up a lot of great facts
Defeating America's Career Politicians. The scoundrels need to go.
Midnight Mass by Jack Lammers… You remember what it was like Great story
The Bike by Jack Lammers… Great heartwarming Story by Jack
Wipe Out All Student Loan Debt--Now! Watch the economy go boom!
No Free Lunch Pay Back Welfare! Why not pay it back?
Deport All Millennials Now!!! Why they deserve to be deported and/or saved
DELETE the EPA, Please! The worst decisions to hurt America
Taxation Without Representation 4th Edition Should we throw the TEA overboard again?
Four Great Political Essays by Thomas Dawson
Top Ten Political Books for 2018… Cliffnotes Version of 10 Political Books
Top Six Patriotic Books for 2018… Cliffnotes version of 6 Patriotic Books
Why Trump Got Elected!.. It's great to hear about a great milestone in America!
The Day the Free Press Died. Corrupt Press Lives on!
Solved (Immigration) The best solutions for 2018
Solved II (Obamacare, Social Security, Student Debt) Check it out; They're solved.
Great Moments in Pittsburgh Steelers Football... Six Super Bowls and more.
Great Players in Pittsburgh Steelers Football ,,,Chuck Noll, Bill Cowher, Mike Tomin, etc.
Great Coaches in New England Patriots Football,,, Bill Belichick the one and only plus others
Great Players in New England Patriots Football… Tom Brady, Drew Bledsoe et al.
Great Coaches in Philadelphia Eagles Football..Andy Reid, Doug Pederson & Lots more
Great Players in Philadelphia Eagles Football Great players such as Sonny Jurgenson
Great Coaches in Syracuse Football All the greats including Ben Schwartzwalder
Great Players in Syracuse Football. Highlights best players such as Jim Brown & Donovan McNabb
Millennials are People Too !!! Give US millennials help to live American Dream
Brian Kelly for the United States Senate from PA: Fresh Face for US Senate
The Candidate's Bible. Don't pray for your campaign without this bible
Rush Limbaugh's Platform for Americans… Rush will love it

Democrat Secret for Power & Winning Elections

Sean Hannity's Platform for Americans… Sean will love it
Donald Trump's New Platform for Americans. Make Trump unbeatable in 2020
Tariffs Are Good for America! One of the best tools a president can have
Great Coaches in Pittsburgh Steelers Football Sixteen of the best coaches ever to coach in pro football.
Great Moments in New England Patriots Football Great football moments from Boston to New England
Great Moments in Philadelphia Eagles Football. The best from the Eagles from the beginning of football.
Great Moments in Syracuse Football The great moments, coaches & players in Syracuse Football
Boost Social Security Now! Hey Buddy Can You Spare a Dime?
The Birth of American Football. From the first college game in 1869 to the last Super Bowl
Obamacare: A One-Line Repeal Congress must get this done.
A Wilkes-Barre Christmas Story A wonderful town makes Christmas all the better
A Boy, A Bike, A Train, and a Christmas Miracle a Christmas story that will melt your heart
Pay-to-Go   America-First Immigration Fix
Legalizing Illegal Aliens Via Resident Visas Americans-first plan saves $Trillions. Learn how!
60 Million Illegal Aliens in America!!! A simple, America-first solution.
The Bill of Rights by Founder James Madison Refresh *your knowledge of the specific rights for all*
Great Players in Army Football Great Army Football played by great players..
Great Coaches in Army Football Army's coaches are all great.
Great Moments in Army Football Army Football at its best.
Great Moments in Florida Gators Football Gators Football from the start. This is the book.
Great Moments in Clemson Football CU Football at its best. This is the book.
Great Moments in Florida Gators Football Gators Football from the start. This is the book.
The Constitution Companion. A Guide to Reading and Comprehending the Constitution
The Constitution by Hamilton, Jefferson, & Madison – Big type and in English
PATERNO: The Dark Days After Win # 409. Sky began to fall within days of win # 409.
JoePa 409 Victories: Say No More! Winningest Division I-A football coach ever
American College Football: The Beginning From before day one football was played.
Great Coaches in Alabama Football Challenging the coaches of every other program!
Great Coaches in Penn State Football the Best Coaches in PSU's football program
Great Players in Penn State Football The best players in PSU's football program
Great Players in Notre Dame Football The best players in ND's football program
Great Coaches in Notre Dame Football The best coaches in any football program
Great Players in Alabama Football from Quarterbacks to offensive Linemen Greats!
Great Moments in Alabama Football AU Football from the start. This is the book.
Great Moments in Penn State Football PSU Football, start--games, coaches, players,
Great Moments in Notre Dame Football ND Football, start, games, coaches, players
Cross Country with the Parents A great trip from East Coast to West with the kids
Seniors, Social Security & the Minimum Wage. Things seniors need to know.
How to Write Your First Book and Publish It with CreateSpace. You too can be an author.
The US Immigration Fix--It's all in here. Finally, an answer.
I had a Dream IBM Could be #1 Again The title is self-explanatory
WineDiets.Com Presents The Wine Diet Learn how to lose weight while having fun.
Wilkes-Barre, PA; Return to Glory Wilkes-Barre City's return to glory
Geoffrey Parsons' Epoch... The Land of Fair Play Better than the original.
The Bill of Rights 4 Dummmies! This is the best book to learn about your rights.
Sol Bloom's Epoch …Story of the Constitution The best book to learn the Constitution
America 4 Dummmies! All Americans should read to learn about this great country.
The Electoral College 4 Dummmies! How does it really work?
The All-Everything Machine Story about IBM's finest computer server.
Thank You IBM! This book explains how IBM was beaten in the computer marketplace by neophytes

Amazon.com/author/brianwkelly
Brian W. Kelly has written 195 books including this one.
Thank you for buying this one.
Others can be found at amazon.com/author/brianwkelly

www.ingramcontent.com/pod-product-compliance
Lightning Source LLC
Chambersburg PA
CBHW022337280326
41934CB00006B/665